THE LIBRARY
COLLEGE
DON

National Health Service Reform and Health Care Professions Act 2002

CHAPTER 17

This book is to be returned on or before the last date

FOR

NATIONAL HEALTH SERVICE, LIC

THE LIBRARY
NEW COLLEGE
SWINDON

National Health Service Reform and Health Care Professions Act 2002

2002 CHAPTER 17

An Act to amend the law about the national health service; to establish and make provision in connection with a Commission for Patient and Public Involvement in Health; to make provision in relation to arrangements for joint working between NHS bodies and the prison service, and between NHS bodies and local authorities in Wales; to make provision in connection with the regulation of health care professions; and for connected purposes.

[25th June 2002]

B E IT ENACTED by the Queen's most Excellent Majesty, by and with the advice and consent of the Lords Spiritual and Temporal, and Commons, in this present Parliament assembled, and by the authority of the same, as follows:—

PART 1

NATIONAL HEALTH SERVICE, ETC

NHS bodies and their functions: England

1 English Health Authorities: change of name

(1) On and after the date on which this section comes into force, Health Authorities for areas in England are to be known instead as Strategic Health Authorities.

(2) Accordingly, for section 8 of the National Health Service Act 1977 (c. 49) (in this Act referred to as "the 1977 Act") (establishment and abolition of Health Authorities) there is substituted —

"8   Health Authorities and Strategic Health Authorities

(1)   It is the duty of the Secretary of State to establish, in accordance with Part 1 of Schedule 5 to this Act, authorities to be called —

    (a)   Strategic Health Authorities, in the case of authorities established for areas in England;

    (b)   Health Authorities, in the case of authorities established for areas in Wales.

(2)   Subject to subsection (4) below —

    (a)   a Strategic Health Authority shall be established for such area of England as is specified in the order establishing the authority; and

    (b)   a Health Authority shall be established for such area of Wales as is so specified, or, if the order so provides, for the whole of Wales.

(3)   A Strategic Health Authority or a Health Authority shall be known by such name, in addition to the title "Strategic Health Authority" or "Health Authority", as —

    (a)   appears to the Secretary of State appropriately to signify the connection of the authority with the area for which they are established; and

    (b)   is specified in the order establishing the authority.

(4)   The Secretary of State may by order —

    (a)   vary the area of a Strategic Health Authority or Health Authority;

    (b)   abolish a Strategic Health Authority or Health Authority;

    (c)   establish a new Strategic Health Authority or Health Authority;

    (d)   change the name by which a Strategic Health Authority or Health Authority are known.

(5)   No order shall be made under this section relating to a Strategic Health Authority until after the completion of such consultation as may be prescribed.

(6)   Consultation requirements contained in regulations under subsection (5) are in addition to, and not in substitution for, any other consultation requirements which may apply.

(7)   The Secretary of State shall act under this section so as to ensure —

    (a)   that the areas for which Strategic Health Authorities are at any time established together comprise the whole of England;

    (b)   that the areas for which Health Authorities are at any time established together comprise the whole of Wales; and

    (c)   that no area for which a Strategic Health Authority or a Health Authority are established extends both into England and into Wales.

(8)   The power to make incidental or supplemental provision conferred by section 126(4) below includes, in particular, in its application to orders made under this section, power to make provision for the transfer of staff, property, rights and liabilities."

(3) Schedule 1 (which contains amendments consequential upon this section) is to have effect.

2 Primary Care Trusts

(1) Section 16A of the 1977 Act (which provides for the establishment of Primary Care Trusts) is amended as provided in subsections (2) and (3).

(2) For subsection (1) there is substituted —

> "(1) It is the duty of the Secretary of State to establish bodies to be known as Primary Care Trusts for areas in England with a view to their exercising functions in relation to the health service.
>
> (1A) The Secretary of State shall act under this section so as to ensure that the areas for which Primary Care Trusts are at any time established together comprise the whole of England."

(3) In subsection (3), after "the area" there is inserted "of England".

(4) Schedule 5A to the 1977 Act (which makes further provision about Primary Care Trusts) is amended as follows —

    (a) in paragraph 2(3) —

        (i) for "the Health Authority in whose area a Primary Care Trust is established to meet the costs" there is substituted "a Strategic Health Authority whose area includes any part of the area of a Primary Care Trust to meet costs", and

        (ii) in paragraph (b), after "meet" there is inserted "(or to contribute towards its meeting)",

    (b) in paragraph 2(4), for "the Health Authority in whose area a Primary Care Trust is established" there is substituted "a Strategic Health Authority whose area includes any part of the area of a Primary Care Trust",

    (c) in paragraph 16(1), for "the Health Authority within whose area the trust's area falls" there is substituted "each Strategic Health Authority whose area includes any part of the trust's area", and

    (d) in paragraph 16(3), for "the Health Authority within whose area the trust's area falls" there is substituted "any Strategic Health Authority whose area includes any part of the trust's area".

(5) Schedule 2 (which contains amendments of the 1977 Act and of other enactments to reallocate functions of Health Authorities to Primary Care Trusts and to make certain connected amendments) is to have effect.

3 Directions: distribution of functions

(1) The 1977 Act is amended as follows.

(2) In section 16D (Secretary of State's directions: distribution of functions), in subsection (1), after "Special Health Authority" there is inserted "or a Primary Care Trust".

(3) For section 17A (Health Authority's directions: distribution of functions) there is substituted —

"17A   Strategic Health Authority's directions: distribution of functions

(1)   A Strategic Health Authority may, in relation to any specified functions of theirs, direct a Primary Care Trust any part of whose area falls within their area to exercise those functions.

(2)   But a Strategic Health Authority may not so direct a Primary Care Trust in relation to any functions of the Strategic Health Authority arising under section 28C arrangements if the Primary Care Trust is providing any services in accordance with those arrangements.

(3)   The Secretary of State may direct Strategic Health Authorities that specified functions of theirs –

     (a)   are to be exercisable, or exercisable to (or only to) any specified extent, by Primary Care Trusts; or

     (b)   are not to be exercisable by Primary Care Trusts,

and that the power in subsection (1) above is to be exercised accordingly.

(4)   Directions under subsection (3)(a) above may include directions that any of the specified functions are to be exercised (or exercised to or only to any specified extent) jointly with the Strategic Health Authority, or jointly by one or more Primary Care Trusts; but such directions may be given only if regulations providing for the joint exercise of those functions have been made under section 16 or 16B above.

(5)   In this section, "specified" means specified in the directions."

(4)   In section 17B (Health Authority's directions: exercise of functions), in subsection (1), the words from "which" to the end are omitted.

(5)   In section 18 (directions and regulations under preceding provisions), in subsection (1A) –

     (a)   "or" is inserted after paragraph (a),

     (b)   paragraph (b) is omitted, and

     (c)   in paragraph (c), for "16D, 17 or 17A" there is substituted "16D or 17".

4   Personal medical services, personal dental services and local pharmaceutical services

(1)   In section 9 of the National Health Service (Primary Care) Act 1997 (c. 46) (relationship between Part 1 of that Act and the 1977 Act), after subsection (1) there is inserted –

"(1A)   In subsection (1), the words from ", apart from" to "functions)," have effect only in relation to Wales."

(2)   In section 36 of the Health and Social Care Act 2001 (c. 15) (effect of the 1977 Act), after subsection (1) there is inserted –

"(1A)   In subsection (1), the words from ", apart from" to "authority)," have effect only in relation to Wales."

(3)   Schedule 3 (which contains amendments of the National Health Service (Primary Care) Act 1997 and of other enactments related to the provisions of this section and sections 1 to 3) is to have effect.

5   Local Representative Committees

(1)   Section 44 of the 1977 Act (recognition of local representative committees) is amended in accordance with subsections (2) to (7).

(2)   Before subsection (A1) there is inserted—

"(ZA1)   A Primary Care Trust may recognise a committee formed for its area, or for the area of that and one or more other Primary Care Trusts, which it is satisfied is representative of—

    (a)   the medical practitioners providing general medical services or general ophthalmic services in the Primary Care Trust's area;

    (b)   those medical practitioners and the deputy medical practitioners for the Primary Care Trust's area;

    (c)   the medical practitioners mentioned in—

        (i)   paragraph (a) above; or

        (ii)   paragraph (b) above,

and the section 28C medical practitioners for the Primary Care Trust's area,

and any committee so recognised shall be called the Local Medical Committee for the Primary Care Trust's area."

(3)   After subsection (A1) there is inserted—

"(A2)   A Primary Care Trust may recognise a committee formed for its area, or for the area of that and one or more other Primary Care Trusts, which it is satisfied is representative of—

    (a)   the dental practitioners providing general dental services in the Primary Care Trust's area;

    (b)   those dental practitioners and the deputy dental practitioners for the Primary Care Trust's area;

    (c)   the dental practitioners mentioned in—

        (i)   paragraph (a) above; or

        (ii)   paragraph (b) above,

and the section 28C dental practitioners for the Primary Care Trust's area,

and any committee so recognised shall be called the Local Dental Committee for the Primary Care Trust's area."

(4)   After subsection (B1) there is inserted—

"(B2)   Where a Primary Care Trust is satisfied that a committee formed for its area, or for its area together with the area of one or more other Primary Care Trusts, is representative—

    (a)   of the ophthalmic opticians providing general ophthalmic services in the Primary Care Trust's area; or

    (b)   of the persons providing pharmaceutical services from premises in the Primary Care Trust's area,

the Primary Care Trust may recognise that committee; and any committee so recognised shall be called the Local Optical Committee or the Local Pharmaceutical Committee, as the case may be, for the area of the Primary Care Trust."

(5)   In subsection (2), "with the approval of the Health Authority" is omitted.

(6)   In subsection (3) —

     (a)   in each of paragraphs (a) and (c), before "Health Authority" there is inserted "Primary Care Trust or",

     (b)   after paragraph (a) there is inserted —

         "(aa)   is a section 28C medical practitioner for the area of a Primary Care Trust if he is a medical practitioner who performs personal medical services in the area of the Primary Care Trust in accordance with arrangements made under section 28C above;", and

     (c)   after paragraph (c) there is inserted —

         "(ca)   is a section 28C dental practitioner for the area of a Primary Care Trust if he is a dental practitioner who performs personal dental services in the area of the Primary Care Trust in accordance with arrangements made under section 28C above;".

(7)   In subsection (4), after "notified the" there is inserted "Primary Care Trust or".

(8)   Section 45 of the 1977 Act (functions of local representative committees) is amended as follows.

(9)   After subsection (1) there is inserted —

     "(1ZA)   Regulations may require —

         (a)   Primary Care Trusts, in the exercise of their functions under this Part of this Act, to consult committees recognised by them under section 44 above,

         (b)   Strategic Health Authorities, in the exercise of any of their functions which relate to arrangements under section 28C above, to consult committees recognised under section 44(ZA1)(c) or (A2)(c) above by Primary Care Trusts for the area or areas where the personal medical or dental services are provided (or to be provided) under the arrangements,

     on such occasions and to such extent as may be prescribed."

(10)   In subsection (1A) —

     (a)   for "power conferred by subsection (1) above is" there is substituted "powers conferred by subsections (1) and (1ZA) above are", and

     (b)   after "require a" there is inserted "Strategic Health Authority, Primary Care Trust or".

(11)   In subsection (1C) —

     (a)   for "subsection (A1)(b) or (c) or (B1)(b) or (c)" there is substituted "subsection (ZA1)(b) or (c), (A1)(b) or (c), (A2)(b) or (c) or (B1)(b) or (c)",

     (b)   before paragraph (a) there is inserted —

         "(za)   in the case of a committee recognised under subsection (ZA1)(b) or (c)(ii) of that section, to the deputy medical practitioners for the Primary Care Trust's area;

         (zb)   in the case of a committee recognised under subsection (ZA1)(c) of that section, to the section 28C medical practitioners for that area;", and

     (c)   after paragraph (b) there is inserted —

> "(ba) in the case of a committee recognised under subsection (A2)(b) or (c)(ii) of that section, to the deputy dental practitioners for the Primary Care Trust's area;
>
> (bb) in the case of a committee recognised under subsection (A2)(c) of that section, to the section 28C dental practitioners for that area;".

(12) In each of subsections (2) and (3), before "Health Authority", in each place where it occurs, there is inserted "Primary Care Trust or".

NHS bodies and their functions: Wales

6 Local Health Boards

(1) After section 16B of the 1977 Act there is inserted —

"16BA Local Health Boards

(1) The National Assembly for Wales may establish bodies to be known as Local Health Boards with a view, in particular, to their exercising —

    (a) functions of Health Authorities transferred or to be transferred to the Assembly by order under section 27 of the Government of Wales Act 1998 (reform of Welsh health authorities),

    (b) other functions of the Assembly relating to the health service.

(2) Each Local Health Board shall be established by order made by the Assembly (referred to in this Act as an LHB order), and an order may establish more than one Local Health Board.

(3) A Local Health Board shall be established for the area of Wales specified in its LHB order.

(4) If any consultation requirements apply, they must be complied with before an LHB order is varied or revoked.

(5) In this section, "consultation requirements" means requirements about consultation contained in regulations made by the Assembly.

(6) Schedule 5B to this Act (which makes further provision about Local Health Boards) shall have effect.

16BB Local Health Boards: functions

(1) The National Assembly for Wales may direct a Local Health Board to exercise in relation to its area any functions which —

    (a) were exercised by a Health Authority in relation to any part of the same area, and

    (b) have been transferred to the Assembly as mentioned in section 16BA(1) above.

(2) The Assembly may also direct a Local Health Board to exercise in relation to its area such other functions of the Assembly relating to the health service as are specified in the directions.

(3) The functions which may be specified in directions under this section include functions under enactments relating to mental health and nursing homes.

(4) The Assembly may give directions to a Local Health Board about its exercise of any functions.

(5) Directions under subsection (1) above must be given in regulations made by the Assembly; but other directions under this section and directions under section 16BC below may be given in such regulations or by instrument in writing.

16BC Exercise of functions by Local Health Boards

(1) This section applies to functions which are exercisable by a Local Health Board under or by virtue of section 16BB above or this section.

(2) The Assembly may give directions providing for any functions to which this section applies to be exercised –

    (a) by another Local Health Board;

    (b) by a Special Health Authority; or

    (c) jointly with any one or more of the following: Health Authorities, NHS trusts, Primary Care Trusts and other Local Health Boards.

(3) Directions given by the Assembly may provide –

    (a) for any functions to which this section applies to be exercised, on behalf of the Local Health Board by whom they are exercisable, by a committee, sub-committee or officer of the Board,

    (b) for any functions which, under this section, are exercisable by a Special Health Authority to be exercised, on behalf of that authority, by a committee, sub-committee or officer of the authority,

    (c) for any functions which, under this section, are exercisable by a Local Health Board jointly with one or more Health Authorities or other Local Health Boards (but not with any NHS trusts) to be exercised, on behalf of the health service bodies in question, by a joint committee or joint sub-committee."

(2) Schedule 4 (which inserts the new Schedule 5B in the 1977 Act) and Schedule 5 (which makes other amendments relating to Local Health Boards) are to have effect.

(3) In section 126 of the 1977 Act (orders, regulations and directions) –

    (a) in subsection (1) –

        (i) after "PCT order" there is inserted "or an instrument made by the National Assembly for Wales", and

        (ii) in paragraph (b), after "Schedule 5A to this Act" there is inserted ", paragraph 19, 20 or 22 of Schedule 5B to this Act",

    (b) in subsection (3B), after "pursuance of" there is inserted "section 16BB or",

    (c) in subsection (4), for "section 18" there is substituted "section 16BB, 18", and

    (d) in subsection (4A) –

      (i)   the word "or" at the end of paragraph (b) is omitted, and

      (ii)   after paragraph (b) there is inserted –

           "(ba)   paragraph 9(3) of Schedule 5B to this Act, or".

(4)   Section 1 of the National Health Service (Private Finance) Act 1997 (c. 56) (powers to enter into externally financed development agreements) applies to Local Health Boards as it applies to NHS trusts.

Financial arrangements: England and Wales

7   Funding of Strategic Health Authorities and Health Authorities

(1)   Section 97 of the 1977 Act (means of meeting expenditure of Health Authorities etc out of public funds) is amended as follows.

(2)   Before subsection (1) there is inserted –

    "(A1)   It is the duty of the Secretary of State to pay in respect of each financial year to each Strategic Health Authority sums not exceeding the amount allotted for that year by the Secretary of State to the Authority towards meeting the expenditure of the Authority which is attributable to the performance by the Authority of their functions in that year."

(3)   In subsection (3C), after "any year" there is inserted "to a Strategic Health Authority under subsection (A1) above or".

(4)   In subsection (3D), after "given to" there is inserted "the Strategic Health Authority or".

(5)   In subsection (3F), after "any year to" there is inserted "a Strategic Health Authority or".

(6)   In subsection (5), after "allotted to a" there is inserted "Strategic Health Authority,".

(7)   In subsection (6) –

    (a)   after "directions to a" there is inserted "Strategic Health Authority,",

    (b)   at the end of paragraph (a) there is inserted "or", and

    (c)   paragraphs (bb) and (c) are omitted.

(8)   Subsection (8) is omitted.

(9)   In subsection (9), after "paid to" there is inserted "Strategic Health Authorities,".

8   Funding of Primary Care Trusts

For section 97C of the 1977 Act (public funding of Primary Care Trusts) there is substituted –

"97C Public funding of Primary Care Trusts

(1)   It is the duty of the Secretary of State, in respect of each financial year, to pay to each Primary Care Trust –

    (a)   sums equal to their general Part 2 expenditure; and

(b)   sums not exceeding the amount allotted by the Secretary of State to the Primary Care Trust for that year towards meeting the Trust's main expenditure in that year.

(2)   In determining the amount to be allotted for any year to a Primary Care Trust under subsection (1)(b) above (or in varying the amount under subsection (7) below), the Secretary of State may take into account, in whatever way he thinks appropriate—

(a)   the Trust's general Part 2 expenditure; and

(b)   expenditure which would have been the Trust's general Part 2 expenditure but for an order under section 103(1) below,

during any period he thinks appropriate (or such elements of that expenditure as he thinks appropriate).

(3)   Where the Secretary of State has made an initial determination of the amount ("the initial amount") to be allotted for any year to a Primary Care Trust under subsection (1)(b) above, he may increase the initial amount by a further sum if it appears to him that over a period notified to the Trust—

(a)   it satisfied any objectives notified to it as objectives to be met in performing its functions; or

(b)   it performed well against any criteria notified to it as criteria relevant to the satisfactory performance of its functions (whether or not the method of measuring its performance against those criteria was also notified to it).

(4)   In subsection (3) above, "notified" means specified or referred to in a notice given to the Primary Care Trust by the Secretary of State.

(5)   In making any increase under subsection (3) above, the Secretary of State may (whether by directions under subsection (8) below or otherwise) impose any conditions he thinks fit on the application or retention by the Primary Care Trust of the sum in question.

(6)   Where the Secretary of State has, under subsection (3) above, increased by any sum the amount to be allotted for any year to a Primary Care Trust and notified the Trust of the allotment and it subsequently appears to him that the Trust has failed (wholly or in part) to satisfy any conditions imposed in making that increase, he may—

(a)   reduce the allotment made to the Trust for that year; or

(b)   when he has made an initial determination of the amount ("the initial amount") to be allotted for any subsequent year to the Trust under subsection (1)(b) above, reduce the initial amount,

by any amount not exceeding that sum.

(7)   An amount is allotted to a Primary Care Trust for a year under this section when the Trust is notified by the Secretary of State that the amount is allotted to the Trust for that year; and the Secretary of State may make an allotment under this section increasing or reducing (subject to subsection (6) above) an allotment previously so made, and the reference to a determination in subsection (3) above includes a determination made with a view to increasing or reducing an allotment previously so made.

(8)   The Secretary of State may give directions to a Primary Care Trust with respect to—

(a) the application of sums paid to it under this section, or

(b) the payment of sums by it to the Secretary of State in respect of charges or other sums referable to the valuation or disposal of assets.

(9) Sums falling to be paid to Primary Care Trusts under this section shall be payable subject to compliance with such conditions as to records, certificates or otherwise as the Secretary of State may determine."

9   Funding of Local Health Boards

(1) After section 97E of the 1977 Act there is inserted —

"97F   Public funding of Local Health Boards

(1) It is the duty of the National Assembly for Wales, in respect of each financial year, to pay to each Local Health Board —

(a) sums equal to their general Part 2 expenditure; and

(b) sums not exceeding the amount allotted by the National Assembly for Wales to the Local Health Board for that year towards meeting the Board's main expenditure in that year.

(2) In determining the amount to be allotted for any year to a Local Health Board under subsection (1)(b) above (or in varying the amount under subsection (7) below), the National Assembly for Wales may take into account, in whatever way the Assembly thinks appropriate —

(a) the Board's general Part 2 expenditure; and

(b) expenditure which would have been the Board's general Part 2 expenditure but for an order under section 103(1) below,

during any period the Assembly thinks appropriate (or such elements of that expenditure as it thinks appropriate).

(3) Where the National Assembly for Wales has made an initial determination of the amount ("the initial amount") to be allotted for any year to a Local Health Board under subsection (1)(b) above, the Assembly may increase the initial amount by a further sum if it appears to it that over a period notified to the Board —

(a) the Board satisfied any objectives notified to it as objectives to be met in performing its functions; or

(b) it performed well against any criteria notified to it as criteria relevant to the satisfactory performance of its functions (whether or not the method of measuring its performance against those criteria was also notified to it).

(4) In subsection (3) above, "notified" means specified or referred to in a notice given to the Local Health Board by the National Assembly for Wales.

(5) In making any increase under subsection (3) above, the National Assembly for Wales may (whether by directions under subsection (8) below or otherwise) impose any conditions it thinks fit on the application or retention by the Local Health Board of the sum in question.

(6)   Where the National Assembly for Wales has, under subsection (3) above, increased by any sum the amount to be allotted for any year to a Local Health Board and notified the Board of the allotment and it subsequently appears to the Assembly that the Board has failed (wholly or in part) to satisfy any conditions imposed in making that increase, the Assembly may —

    (a)   reduce the allotment made to the Board for that year; or

    (b)   when the Assembly has made an initial determination of the amount ("the initial amount") to be allotted for any subsequent year to the Board under subsection (1)(b) above, reduce the initial amount,

by any amount not exceeding that sum.

(7)   An amount is allotted to a Local Health Board for a year under this section when the Board is notified by the National Assembly for Wales that the amount is allotted to the Board for that year; and the National Assembly for Wales may make an allotment under this section increasing or reducing (subject to subsection (6) above) an allotment previously so made, and the reference to a determination in subsection (3) above includes a determination made with a view to increasing or reducing an allotment previously so made.

(8)   The National Assembly for Wales may give directions to a Local Health Board with respect to —

    (a)   the application of sums paid to the Board under this section, or

    (b)   the payment of sums by the Board to the National Assembly for Wales in respect of charges or other sums referable to the valuation or disposal of assets.

(9)   Sums falling to be paid to Local Health Boards under this section shall be payable subject to compliance with such conditions as to records, certificates or otherwise as the National Assembly for Wales may determine.

97G   Financial duties of Local Health Boards

(1)   It is the duty of every Local Health Board, in respect of each financial year, to perform its functions so as to secure that the expenditure of the Board which is attributable to the performance by the Board of its functions in that year (not including expenditure within subsection (1)(a) of section 97F above) does not exceed the aggregate of —

    (a)   the amount allotted to it for that year under subsection (1)(b) of that section;

    (b)   any sums received by it in that year under any provision of this Act (other than sums received by it under that section); and

    (c)   any sums received by it in that year otherwise than under this Act for the purpose of enabling it to defray any such expenditure.

(2)   The National Assembly for Wales may give such directions to a Local Health Board as appear to be requisite to secure that the Board complies with the duty imposed on it by subsection (1) above.

(3)   Directions under subsection (2) may be specific in character.

(4)   To the extent to which —

(a) any expenditure is defrayed by a Local Health Board as trustee or on behalf of a Local Health Board by special trustees; or

(b) any sums are received by a Local Health Board as trustee or under section 96A above,

that expenditure and, subject to subsection (6) below, those sums shall be disregarded for the purposes of this section.

(5) For the purposes of this section sums which, in the hands of a Local Health Board, cease to be trust funds and become applicable by the Local Health Board otherwise than as trustee shall be treated, on their becoming so applicable, as having been received by the Local Health Board otherwise than as trustee.

(6) Of the sums received by a Local Health Board under section 96A above so much only as accrues to the Local Health Board after defraying any expenses incurred in obtaining them shall be disregarded under subsection (4) above.

(7) Subject to subsection (4) above, the National Assembly for Wales may by directions determine—

(a) whether specified sums are, or are not, to be treated for the purposes of this section as received under this Act by a specified Local Health Board;

(b) whether specified expenditure is, or is not, to be treated for those purposes as expenditure within subsection (1) above of a specified Local Health Board; or

(c) the extent to which, and the circumstances in which, sums received by a Local Health Board under section 97F above but not yet spent are to be treated for the purposes of this section as part of the expenditure of the Local Health Board and to which financial year's expenditure they are to be attributed.

(8) In subsection (7) above, "specified" means of a description specified in the directions.

97H Resource limits for Local Health Boards

(1) It is the duty of every Local Health Board to ensure that the use of its resources in a financial year does not exceed the amount specified for it in relation to that year by the National Assembly for Wales.

(2) For the purpose of subsection (1) above no account shall be taken of any use of resources for the purposes of a Board's general Part 2 expenditure (within the meaning of paragraph 6A of Schedule 12A).

(3) But in specifying an amount for a Local Health Board under subsection (1) above (or in varying the amount under subsection (5) below), the National Assembly for Wales may take into account (in whatever way it thinks appropriate)—

(a) any such use of resources; and

(b) the use of any resources which would have been for the purpose of the Board's general Part 2 expenditure but for an order under section 103(1) below,

during any period the Assembly thinks appropriate (or such elements of such uses of resources as it thinks appropriate).

(4)   For the purpose of subsection (1) above the National Assembly for Wales may give directions—

    (a)   specifying uses of resources which are to be, or not to be, taken into account;

    (b)   making provision for determining to which Local Health Board certain uses of resources are to be attributed;

    (c)   specifying descriptions of resources which are to be, or not to be, taken into account.

(5)   Where an amount has been specified under this section in respect of a financial year, it may be varied by a later specification.

(6)   Subsections (4) to (6) of section 97G above shall apply in relation to the duty under subsection (1) above as they apply in relation to the duty under section 97G(1); and for that purpose references to the defraying of expenditure and the receipt of sums shall be construed as references to the incurring of liabilities and the acquisition of assets.

(7)   The provisions in section 97G(2) and (3) above about the giving of directions by the National Assembly for Wales shall apply in relation to the duty under subsection (1) above as they apply in relation to the duty under section 97G(1).

(8)   In this section a reference to the use of resources is a reference to their expenditure, consumption or reduction in value."

10   Expenditure of NHS bodies

(1)   The 1977 Act is amended as follows.

(2)   In section 97 (means of meeting expenditure of Health Authorities etc out of public funds), in subsection (3BB), for "section 97C" there is substituted "sections 97C and 97F".

(3)   Schedule 12A to the 1977 Act (expenditure of Health Authorities and Primary Care Trusts) is amended as follows.

(4)   In paragraph 3—

    (a)   in each of sub-paragraphs (1), (4) and (5), for "Secretary of State" there is substituted "National Assembly for Wales",

    (b)   in sub-paragraph (1), for "he" there is substituted "it",

    (c)   in sub-paragraph (4)—

        (i)   for "his discretion" there is substituted "its discretion", and

        (ii)   for "his opinion" there is substituted "the Assembly's opinion", and

    (d)   in sub-paragraph (5), for "he" there is substituted "the Assembly".

(5)   In paragraph 4(2), the word "or" at the end of paragraph (a) is omitted, and after paragraph (a) there is inserted—

    "(aa)   remuneration referable to the cost of drugs,

    (ab)   remuneration paid to persons providing additional pharmaceutical services (in accordance with directions under section 41A above), in respect of such of those services as are designated, or".

(6)   In paragraph 5(1)—

    (a)   the "and" at the end of paragraph (a) is omitted,

    (b)   in paragraph (b), for "(other than general Part II expenditure)," there is substituted "(other than general Part 2 expenditure and remuneration referable to the cost of drugs), and", and

    (c)   for the words following paragraph (b) there is substituted —

        "(c)   expenditure attributable to remuneration referable to the cost of drugs for which the trust is accountable in that year (whether paid by it or by another trust)."

(7)   In paragraph 5(2), the "or" at the end of paragraph (a) is omitted, and after paragraph (a) there is inserted —

        "(aa)   remuneration paid in that year to persons providing additional pharmaceutical services (in accordance with directions under section 41A above), in respect of such of those services as are designated, or".

(8)   For paragraph 6 there is substituted —

    "6   (1)   For each financial year, the Secretary of State shall apportion, in such manner as he thinks appropriate, among all Primary Care Trusts the total of the remuneration referable to the cost of drugs which is paid by each Primary Care Trust in that year.

        (2)   A Primary Care Trust is accountable in any year for remuneration referable to the cost of drugs to the extent (and only to the extent) that such remuneration is apportioned to it under sub-paragraph (1) above.

        (3)   Where in any financial year any remuneration referable to the cost of drugs for which a Primary Care Trust is accountable is paid by another Primary Care Trust, the remuneration is to be treated (for the purposes of sections 97C and 97D above) as having been paid by the first trust in the performance of its functions.

        (4)   The Secretary of State may, in particular, exercise his discretion under sub-paragraph (1) above —

           (a)   so that any apportionment reflects, in the case of each Primary Care Trust, the financial consequences of orders for the provision of drugs, being orders which in his opinion are attributable to the trust in question,

           (b)   by reference to averaged or estimated amounts.

        (5)   The Secretary of State may make provision for any remuneration referable to the cost of drugs which is paid by a Primary Care Trust other than the trust which is accountable for the payment to be reimbursed in such manner as he may determine."

(9)   After paragraph 6 there is inserted —

"Local Health Boards: general Part 2 expenditure

    6A   (1)   In section 97F above and this Schedule, general Part 2 expenditure, in relation to a Local Health Board, means expenditure of the Board which —

           (a)   is attributable to the payment of remuneration to persons providing services in pursuance of Part 2 of this Act, and

           (b)   is not excluded by sub-paragraph (2) below.

(2) Expenditure is excluded if it is attributable to—

    (a) the reimbursement of expenses of persons providing services in pursuance of Part 2 which are designated expenses incurred in connection with the provision of the services (or in giving instruction in matters relating to the services),

    (b) remuneration referable to the cost of drugs,

    (c) remuneration paid to persons providing additional pharmaceutical services (in accordance with directions under section 41A above), in respect of such of those services as are designated, or

    (d) remuneration of a designated description which is determined by the Board and paid to persons providing general medical services in pursuance of Part 2.

Local Health Boards: main expenditure

6B (1) In section 97F above, main expenditure, in relation to a Local Health Board and the year in question, means—

    (a) expenditure of the Board mentioned in sub-paragraph (2) below,

    (b) any other expenditure of the Board attributable to the performance of its functions in that year (other than general Part 2 expenditure and remuneration referable to the cost of drugs), and

    (c) expenditure attributable to remuneration referable to the cost of drugs for which the Board is accountable in that year (whether paid by it or by another Board).

  (2) The expenditure referred to in sub-paragraph (1)(a) above is expenditure attributable to—

    (a) the reimbursement in that year of expenses of persons providing services in pursuance of Part 2 which are designated expenses incurred in connection with the provision of the services (or in giving instruction in matters relating to the services),

    (b) remuneration paid in that year to persons providing additional pharmaceutical services (in accordance with directions under section 41A above), in respect of such of those services as are designated, or

    (c) remuneration of a designated description which is determined by the Board and paid in that year to persons providing general medical services in pursuance of Part 2.

6C (1) For each financial year, the National Assembly for Wales shall apportion, in such manner as it thinks appropriate, among all Local Health Boards the total of the remuneration referable to the cost of drugs which is paid by each Local Health Board in that year.

  (2) A Local Health Board is accountable in any year for remuneration referable to the cost of drugs to the extent (and only to the extent) that such remuneration is apportioned to it under sub-paragraph (1) above.

  (3) Where in any financial year any remuneration referable to the cost of drugs for which a Local Health Board is accountable is paid by another Local Health Board, the remuneration is to be treated (for the

purposes of sections 97F and 97G above) as having been paid by the first Board in the performance of its functions.

    (4) The National Assembly for Wales may, in particular, exercise its discretion under sub-paragraph (1) above—

        (a) so that any apportionment reflects, in the case of each Local Health Board, the financial consequences of orders for the provision of drugs, being orders which in the Assembly's opinion are attributable to the Board in question,

        (b) by reference to averaged or estimated amounts.

    (5) The National Assembly for Wales may make provision for any remuneration referable to the cost of drugs which is paid by a Local Health Board other than the Board which is accountable for the payment to be reimbursed in such manner as the Assembly may determine."

  (10) In paragraph 7—

    (a) in sub-paragraph (1)—

        (i) in the definition of "designated", after "Secretary of State" there is inserted "or, as the case may be, the National Assembly for Wales", and

        (ii) in the definition of "remuneration referable to the cost of drugs", for "paragraph 1(2)(b)" there is substituted "paragraphs 1(2)(b), 4(2)(aa) and 6A(2)(b)",

    (b) in sub-paragraph (2), for "Health Authorities" there is substituted "Primary Care Trusts", and at the end there is inserted "and the National Assembly for Wales shall make the corresponding determination in relation to Health Authorities and Local Health Boards.", and

    (c) in sub-paragraph (3)—

        (i) for "Health Authorities" there is substituted "Primary Care Trusts",

        (ii) "or Primary Care Trust" is omitted, and

        (iii) at the end there is inserted ", and the National Assembly for Wales may so treat all remuneration paid by Health Authorities to such persons, so far as it is so met."

Quality

11 Duty of quality

In section 18 of the 1999 Act (duty of quality), in subsection (4), at the end of the definition of "health care" there is inserted ", and the environment in which such services are provided".

12 Further functions of the Commission for Health Improvement

    (1) Section 20 of the 1999 Act (functions of the Commission for Health Improvement) is amended as provided in subsections (2) to (4).

    (2) In subsection (1)—

        (a) in paragraph (d), for "particular types of health care" there is substituted "health care",

(b)   the "and" at the end of paragraph (d) is omitted, and

(c)   after paragraph (d) there is inserted —

"(da)   the function of conducting reviews of, and making reports on, the quality of data obtained by others relating to the management, provision or quality of, or access to or availability of, health care for which NHS bodies or service providers have responsibility, the validity of conclusions drawn from such data, and the methods used in their collection and analysis, ".

(3)   After subsection (1) there is inserted —

"(1A)   The functions of conducting reviews and of carrying out investigations include —

(a)   the collection and analysis of data, and

(b)   the assessment of performance against criteria.

(1B)   Subject to any regulations under paragraph (d) of subsection (2), the Commission must publish at least a summary of each report it makes in the exercise of the functions conferred on it by or under this section and sections 21 and 22."

(4)   In subsection (2), for paragraph (d) there is substituted —

"(d)   as to cases or classes of case in which the Commission must publish reports (and not just summaries),".

(5)   In section 33 of the Audit Commission Act 1998 (c. 18) (studies for improving economy etc in services), in subsection (6)(c), after "Secretary of State" there is inserted ", the Commission for Health Improvement".

13   Commission for Health Improvement: inspections and investigations

(1)   In section 20 of the 1999 Act (functions of the Commission for Health Improvement) —

(a)   in subsection (1), after the paragraph (da) inserted by section 12 there is inserted —

"(db)   the function of carrying out inspections of NHS bodies and service providers, and persons who provide or are to provide health care for which NHS bodies or service providers have responsibility, and making reports on the inspections, and", and

(b)   after the subsections (1A) and (1B) inserted by section 12 there is inserted —

"(1C)   The inspections referred to in paragraph (db) of subsection (1) are to be carried out only in connection with the function referred to in paragraph (d) of that subsection.

(1D)   If after carrying out —

(a)   a review under subsection (1)(b),

(b)   an investigation under subsection (1)(c),

(c)   any function equivalent to one referred to in paragraph (a) or (b) prescribed under subsection (1)(e), or

(d)   an inspection under subsection (1)(db),

the Commission is of the view referred to in subsection (1E) as to a body, service provider or other person reviewed, investigated or inspected (taking account, if appropriate, of any other relevant information the Commission may have), the Commission must make a report of its view to the Secretary of State.

(1E) The view referred to is that—

(a) the health care for which the body or service provider in question has responsibility is of unacceptably poor quality (whether generally or in particular areas), or

(b) there are significant failings in the way the body, service provider or other person is being run (including, where the service provider or other person is an individual, the way his practice is being run).

(1F) In its report, the Commission may recommend to the Secretary of State that he take special measures in relation to the body or service provider in question with a view to improving the health care for which it is responsible or the way the body, service provider or other person (or, as mentioned in subsection (1E)(b), his practice) is being run.

(1G) The report must give the Commission's reasons for its view, and for any recommendation under subsection (1F)."

(2) In section 23 of that Act (powers of the Commission to obtain information)—

(a) in subsection (1)(a), for "NHS premises" there is substituted "relevant premises",

(b) in subsection (2)(d), after "section 20(1)(c)" there is inserted ", (d) or (db), or any functions equivalent to those under section 20(1)(c) prescribed under section 20(1)(e)", and

(c) in subsection (6)—

(i) the definition of "NHS premises" is omitted, and

(ii) after the definition of "prescribed" there is inserted—

" "relevant premises" means—

(a) premises owned or controlled by an NHS body,

(b) premises owned or controlled by a Local Health Board,

(c) premises owned or controlled by a service provider and used for purposes connected with the services provided,

(d) any other premises used for any purpose connected with the provision of health care for which an NHS body, a service provider or a Local Health Board has responsibility,

(and terms used in this definition have the meaning given by section 20(7) (disregarding section 20(8)(b)))."

14 Commission for Health Improvement: constitution

(1) Schedule 2 to the 1999 Act (the Commission for Health Improvement) is amended as follows.

(2)   After paragraph 5 there is inserted —

"5A (1) The Secretary of State may direct a Special Health Authority to exercise —

(a)   his function of appointing the chairman and the other members referred to in paragraph 4(c), and

(b)   any functions conferred on him by regulations under paragraph 5 in relation to the appointment or tenure of office of the chairman and those other members.

(2)   The National Assembly for Wales may direct a Special Health Authority to exercise —

(a)   its function of appointing the member referred to in paragraph 4(b), and

(b)   any functions conferred on it by regulations under paragraph 5 in relation to the appointment or tenure of office of that member.

(3)   If the Secretary of State or the Assembly gives such directions, the 1977 Act has effect as if —

(a)   the directions were directions under section 16D of that Act, and, accordingly,

(b)   the functions were exercisable by the Special Health Authority under section 16D."

(3)   In paragraph 7 (employees) —

(a)   in sub-paragraph (2), the words after "Commission" are omitted, and

(b)   sub-paragraphs (6) and (7) are omitted.

(4)   In paragraph 8 (delegation of functions) —

(a)   the existing text is renumbered as sub-paragraph (1) of that paragraph,

(b)   in that sub-paragraph (1) (as so renumbered), for "a committee" to the end there is substituted —

"(a)   a committee, sub-committee, member or employee of the Commission, or

(b)   any other person.", and

(c)   after sub-paragraph (1) there is inserted —

"(2)   If the Commission arranges for the discharge of any function falling within section 20(1A) of this Act by one or more committees or sub-committees of the Commission, the persons by whom those functions are to be discharged are to be known collectively as "the Office for Information on Health Care Performance".

(3)   If the Commission arranges for the discharge of any function as mentioned in sub-paragraph (1)(b), the arrangements may include provision with respect to the payment of remuneration and allowances to, or amounts in respect of, such persons."

(5)   In paragraph 12 —

(a)   in sub-paragraph (1), for "the exercise of its functions" there is substituted "the way in which the Commission has exercised its functions", and

(b)   after sub-paragraph (1) there is inserted —

"(1A) As soon as possible after the end of each financial year, the Commission must also make a report to the Secretary of State and the National Assembly for Wales on what it has found in relation to NHS bodies and service providers in the course of exercising its functions during the year.

(1B) The Secretary of State must lay before Parliament any reports he receives under sub-paragraphs (1) and (1A).

(1C) The National Assembly for Wales must publish any report it receives under sub-paragraph (1A)."

Patient and public involvement

15 Establishment of Patients' Forums

(1) The Secretary of State shall establish a body to be known as a Patients' Forum —

    (a) for each NHS trust all or most of whose hospitals, establishments and facilities are situated in England, and

    (b) for each Primary Care Trust.

(2) The members of each Patients' Forum are to be appointed by the Commission for Patient and Public Involvement in Health.

(3) A Patients' Forum must —

    (a) monitor and review the range and operation of services provided by, or under arrangements made by, the trust for which it is established,

    (b) obtain the views of patients and their carers about those matters and report on those views to the trust,

    (c) provide advice, and make reports and recommendations, about matters relating to the range and operation of those services to the trust,

    (d) make available to patients and their carers advice and information about those services,

    (e) in prescribed circumstances, perform any prescribed function of the trust with respect to the provision of a service affording assistance to patients and their families and carers,

    (f) carry out such other functions as may be prescribed.

(4) In providing advice or making recommendations under subsection (3)(c), a Patients' Forum must have regard to the views of patients and their carers.

(5) If, in the course of exercising its functions, a Patients' Forum becomes aware of any matter which in its view —

    (a) should be considered by a relevant overview and scrutiny committee, the Forum may refer that matter to the committee,

    (b) should be brought to the attention of the Commission for Patient and Public Involvement in Health, it may refer that matter to the Commission.

(6) Subsection (5) does not prejudice the power of a Patients' Forum to make such other representations or referrals as it thinks fit, to such persons or bodies as it thinks fit, about matters arising in the course of its exercising its functions.

(7) Patients' Forums must in prescribed circumstances —

    (a) co-operate with each other in the exercise of their functions,

   (b) exercise functions jointly with one or more other Forums.

(8) References in subsection (3) to services are references to—

   (a) services provided as part of the health service in England,

   (b) services provided in England in pursuance of section 31 arrangements in relation to the exercise of health-related functions of a local authority, and

   (c) services provided elsewhere (and not as part of the health service in England) in pursuance of section 31 arrangements with a local authority in England.

(9) In this section—

   "carer", in relation to a patient, means a person who provides care for the patient, but who is not employed to do so by any body in the exercise of its functions under any enactment,

   "the health service" has the same meaning as in the 1977 Act,

   "patient" includes (as well as a patient within the meaning of that Act) a person who receives services provided in pursuance of section 31 arrangements in relation to the exercise of health-related functions of a local authority,

   "prescribed" means prescribed by regulations made by the Secretary of State,

   "relevant overview and scrutiny committee", in relation to a Patients' Forum, means any overview and scrutiny committee in relation to which the Primary Care Trust or NHS trust for which the Forum is established is a local NHS body by virtue of regulations made under section 7(4) of the Health and Social Care Act 2001 (c. 15) (including that provision as read with section 8(5) and as applied by section 10(2) of that Act),

   "section 31 arrangements" means arrangements under regulations under section 31 of the 1999 Act (arrangements between NHS bodies and local authorities).

16 Additional functions of PCT Patients' Forums

(1) A Patients' Forum established for a Primary Care Trust (a "PCT Patients' Forum") has the following additional functions—

   (a) providing independent advocacy services to persons in the Trust's area or persons to whom services have been provided by, or under arrangements with, the Trust,

   (b) making available to patients and their carers advice and information about the making of complaints in relation to services provided by or under arrangements with the Trust, and

   (c) representing to persons and bodies which exercise functions in relation to the area of the Trust (including, in particular, any relevant overview and scrutiny committee) the views of members of the public in the Trust's area about matters affecting their health.

(2) In subsection (1), references to services have the meaning given by section 15(8).

(3) It is also the function of a PCT Patients' Forum—

   (a) to promote the involvement of members of the public in the area of the Trust in consultations or processes leading (or potentially leading) to decisions by those mentioned in subsection (4), or the formulation of policies by them, which would or might affect (whether directly or not) the health of those members of the public,

(b) to make available advice and information to such members of the public about such involvement,

(c) to advise those mentioned in subsection (4) about how to encourage such involvement (including, in the case of bodies mentioned in subsection (4) to which section 11 of the Health and Social Care Act 2001 (c. 15) applies, advising them how to comply with the requirements of that section in relation to the area of the Primary Care Trust), and

(d) to monitor how successful those mentioned in subsection (4) are at achieving such involvement.

(4) Those referred to in subsection (3) are—

(a) Strategic Health Authorities whose areas include any part of the area of the Primary Care Trust,

(b) the Primary Care Trust itself,

(c) NHS trusts which provide services to patients in the area of the Primary Care Trust,

(d) other public bodies, and

(e) others providing services to the public or a section of the public.

(5) In section 12 of the Health and Social Care Act 2001 (which inserts a new section 19A concerning independent advocacy services into the 1977 Act), in that new section 19A, after subsection (6) there is inserted—

"(7) The Secretary of State may direct a Patients' Forum established for a Primary Care Trust to exercise any of his functions under this section so far as they relate to independent advocacy services provided to persons in the area of the Primary Care Trust or persons to whom services have been provided by, or under arrangements with, the Trust; and if he does so—

(a) the functions of that Patients' Forum are to be taken to include those functions, but

(b) the Patients' Forum may not make any arrangements with itself under this section."

(6) In this section—

"carer" and "patient" have the same meaning as in section 15,

"independent advocacy services" means services provided under section 19A of the 1977 Act (independent advocacy services),

"relevant overview and scrutiny committee" has the same meaning as in section 15.

17 Entry and inspection of premises

(1) The Secretary of State may make regulations requiring—

(a) Strategic Health Authorities,

(b) Primary Care Trusts,

(c) Health Authorities,

(d) Local Health Boards,

(e) local authorities,

(f)   NHS trusts,

(g)   persons providing services under Part 2 of the 1977 Act or under arrangements under section 28C of that Act, or

(h)   persons providing piloted services under pilot schemes established under section 28 of the Health and Social Care Act 2001 (c. 15) , or providing LP Services under an LPS scheme established under Schedule 8A to the 1977 Act,

to allow members of a Patients' Forum authorised by or under the regulations to enter and inspect, for the purposes of any of the Forum's functions, premises owned or controlled by those referred to in paragraphs (a) to (h).

(2)   The Secretary of State may also make regulations requiring any other person who owns or controls premises where services are provided as mentioned in subsection (1)(g) or (h) to allow members of a Patients' Forum authorised by or under the regulations to enter and inspect the premises for the purposes of any of the Forum's functions.

(3)   The regulations may in particular make provision as to —

(a)   cases and circumstances in which access is to be permitted,

(b)   limitations or conditions to which access is to be subject.

(4)   In subsection (1), "local authorities" has the same meaning as in section 31 of the 1999 Act (arrangements between NHS bodies and local authorities).

18   Annual reports

(1)   Every Patients' Forum must —

(a)   prepare a report in relation to its activities in each financial year, and

(b)   as soon as possible after the end of each financial year, send a copy of its report for that year to the trust for which it is established, and to the persons mentioned in subsection (2).

(2)   Those persons are —

(a)   the Secretary of State,

(b)   the Commission for Patient and Public Involvement in Health,

(c)   each Strategic Health Authority whose area includes —

(i)   any part of the area of the Primary Care Trust for which the Forum is established, or

(ii)   all or most of the hospitals, establishments and facilities of the NHS trust for which the Forum is established,

(d)   any relevant overview and scrutiny committee within the meaning given by section 15.

(3)   A report under this section relating to any year must include details of the arrangements maintained by the Forum in that year for obtaining the views of patients.

(4)   In this section, "financial year", in relation to a Patients' Forum, means —

(a)   the period beginning with the date on which the Forum is established and ending with the next 31st March, and

(b)   each successive period of 12 months ending with 31st March.

19 Supplementary

(1) The Secretary of State may by regulations make further provision in relation to Patients' Forums.

(2) The regulations may in particular make provision as to—

    (a) the appointment of members,

    (b) any qualification or disqualification for membership,

    (c) terms of appointment,

    (d) circumstances in which a person is to cease to be a member or may be suspended,

    (e) the proceedings of Patients' Forums,

    (f) the discharge of any function of a Patients' Forum by a committee of the Forum or by a joint committee appointed with another Forum,

    (g) the appointment, as members of a committee or joint committee, of persons who are not members of the Forum or Forums concerned,

    (h) the funding of Patients' Forums and the provision of premises, other facilities and staff,

    (i) the payment of travelling and other allowances to members of a Patients' Forum or of a committee of a Forum or a joint committee of two or more Forums (including attendance allowances or compensation for loss of remunerative time),

    (j) the preparation by a Patients' Forum of annual accounts, and their inclusion in accounts of the Commission for Patient and Public Involvement in Health,

    (k) the provision of information (including descriptions of information which are or are not to be provided) to a Patients' Forum by an NHS trust, a Primary Care Trust, a Strategic Health Authority, the Commission for Patient and Public Involvement in Health or a person providing independent advocacy services (within the meaning given by section 19A of the 1977 Act),

    (l) the provision of information by a Patients' Forum to another person (including another Forum),

    (m) the referral of matters by a Patients' Forum to a relevant overview and scrutiny committee (within the meaning given by section 15),

    (n) the preparation and publication of reports by Patients' Forums (including the publication of reports under section 18),

    (o) matters to be included in any such report,

    (p) the furnishing and publication by NHS trusts, Primary Care Trusts and Strategic Health Authorities of comments on reports or recommendations of Patients' Forums.

(3) The regulations must secure that the members of a Patients' Forum include—

    (a) at least one person who is a member or representative of a voluntary organisation whose purpose, or one of whose purposes, is to represent the interests of—

        (i) persons for whom services are being provided under the 1977 Act, or

        (ii) persons who provide care for such persons, but who are not employed to do so by any body in the exercise of its functions under any enactment, and

    (b) at least one person for whom services are being or have been provided by the trust for which the Patients' Forum is established.

(4)   The regulations must also secure that the members of a Patients' Forum established for a Primary Care Trust also include—

  (a)   at least one member of the Patients' Forum established for each NHS trust all or most of whose hospitals, establishments and facilities are situated in the area of the Primary Care Trust, and

  (b)   if it appears to the Commission for Patient and Public Involvement in Health that there is a body which represents members of the public in the Primary Care Trust's area in matters relating to their health, at least one person who is a member or representative of that body (or, if there is more than one such body, of any of those bodies).

(5)   The regulations may include provision applying, or corresponding to, any provision of Part 5A of the Local Government Act 1972 (c. 70) (access to meetings and documents), with or without modifications.

(6)   In section 134 of the Mental Health Act 1983 (c. 20) (correspondence of patients), in subsection (3)(e), after "Community Health Council" there is inserted ", a Patients' Forum".

(7)   In Schedule 1 to the Freedom of Information Act 2000 (c. 36) (public authorities for the purposes of the Act), in Part 3 (National Health Service), after paragraph 41 there is inserted—

  "41A   A Patients' Forum established under section 15 of the National Health Service Reform and Health Care Professions Act 2002."

20   The Commission for Patient and Public Involvement in Health

(1)   There shall be a body corporate to be known as the Commission for Patient and Public Involvement in Health ("the Commission") to exercise the functions set out in subsections (2) to (5) (in addition to its function of appointing members of Patients' Forums).

(2)   The Commission has the following functions—

  (a)   advising the Secretary of State, and such bodies as may be prescribed, about arrangements for public involvement in, and consultation on, matters relating to the health service in England,

  (b)   advising the Secretary of State, and such bodies as may be prescribed, about arrangements for the provision in England of independent advocacy services,

  (c)   representing to the Secretary of State and such bodies as may be prescribed, and advising him and them on, the views, as respects the arrangements referred to in paragraphs (a) and (b), of Patients' Forums and those voluntary organisations and other bodies appearing to the Commission to represent the interests of patients of the health service in England and their carers,

  (d)   providing staff to Patients' Forums established for Primary Care Trusts, and advice and assistance to Patients' Forums and facilitating the co-ordination of their activities,

  (e)   advising and assisting providers of independent advocacy services in England,

  (f)   setting quality standards relating to any aspect of —

    (i)   the way Patients' Forums exercise their functions, and

    (ii)   the services provided by independent advocacy services in England,

> monitoring how successfully they meet those standards, and making recommendations to them about how to improve their performance against those standards,

(g)   such other functions in relation to England as may be prescribed.

(3)   It is also the function of the Commission to promote the involvement of members of the public in England in consultations or processes leading (or potentially leading) to decisions by those mentioned in subsection (4), or the formulation of policies by them, which would or might affect (whether directly or not) the health of those members of the public.

(4)   The decisions in question are those made by —

    (a)   health service bodies,

    (b)   other public bodies, and

    (c)   others providing services to the public or a section of the public.

(5)   It is also the function of the Commission —

    (a)   to review the annual reports of Patients' Forums made under section 18, and

    (b)   to make, to the Secretary of State or to such other persons or bodies as the Commission thinks fit, such reports or recommendations as the Commission thinks fit concerning any matters arising from those annual reports.

(6)   If the Commission —

    (a)   becomes aware in the course of exercising its functions of any matter connected with the health service in England which in its opinion gives rise to concerns about the safety or welfare of patients, and

    (b)   is not satisfied that the matter is being dealt with, or about the way it is being dealt with,

the Commission must report the matter to whichever person or body it considers most appropriate (or, if it considers it appropriate to do so, to more than one person or body).

(7)   Bodies to whom the Commission might report a matter include —

    (a)   the regulatory body for the profession of a person working in the health service,

    (b)   the Commission for Health Improvement.

(8)   The Commission may make such charges as it thinks fit for the provision of advice and other services (but this is subject to any prescribed limitation).

(9)   The Secretary of State may by regulations make further provision in relation to the Commission.

(10)   The regulations may, in particular, make provision as to the provision of information (including descriptions of information which are or are not to be provided) to the Commission by a Strategic Health Authority, a Special Health Authority, an NHS trust, a Primary Care Trust, a Patients' Forum or a provider of independent advocacy services.

(11)   Schedule 6 (which makes further provision about the Commission) is to have effect.

(12)   In this section —

       "carer" and "patient" have the same meaning as in section 15, "the health service" has the same meaning as in the 1977 Act, except that it includes services provided in pursuance of section 31 arrangements in relation to the exercise of health-related functions of a local authority,

"health service bodies" means Strategic Health Authorities, Primary Care Trusts and NHS trusts,

"independent advocacy services" means services provided under section 19A of the 1977 Act (independent advocacy services),

"prescribed" means prescribed by regulations made by the Secretary of State,

"section 31 arrangements" means arrangements under regulations under section 31 of the 1999 Act (arrangements between NHS bodies and local authorities).

21   Overview and scrutiny committees

In section 7 of the Health and Social Care Act 2001 (c. 15) (health-related functions of overview and scrutiny committees), in subsection (3)(b), at the end there is inserted "or to the relevant authority".

22   Abolition of Community Health Councils in England

(1) The Community Health Councils established for districts in England under section 20 of the 1977 Act are abolished.

(2) That section shall cease to have effect in its application to the area of any Health Authority established for an area in England and to any Community Health Council established for a district in England.

(3) The Association of Community Health Councils for England and Wales ("ACHCEW") established under paragraph 5 of Schedule 7 to the 1977 Act is also abolished.

(4) The National Assembly for Wales has as respects Wales the same power under that paragraph as it would have if no such body had been established.

(5) The Secretary of State may by order make provision –
   (a) as to the transfer to a person falling within subsection (6), on or after the abolition of a Community Health Council by subsection (1), of any of the rights or liabilities of a person as a member or former member of the Council,
   (b) as to the transfer to a person falling within subsection (6) or to the National Assembly for Wales, on or after the abolition of ACHCEW, of any of the property held, rights enjoyed or liabilities incurred in respect of the functions of ACHCEW by a person as a member or former member of a Community Health Council which was a member of ACHCEW.

(6) The following fall within this subsection –
   (a) the Secretary of State,
   (b) a Health Authority established for an area in England,
   (c) a Special Health Authority,
   (d) an NHS trust,
   (e) a Primary Care Trust.

(7) Before exercising the power conferred by subsection (5)(b) the Secretary of State must consult the National Assembly for Wales.

(8) If section 1 comes into force before this section –

(a) the references to Health Authorities in section 20 of and Schedule 7 to the 1977 Act are to be construed (until this section comes into force) as including references to Strategic Health Authorities, and

(b) the references in this section to Health Authorities established for areas in England are to have effect as references to Strategic Health Authorities.

(9) If this section comes into force before section 1, the reference in subsection (6)(b) to a Health Authority established for an area in England is to be construed, after section 1 comes into force, as a reference to a Strategic Health Authority.

Joint working

23 Joint working with the prison service

(1) In exercising their respective functions, NHS bodies (on the one hand) and the prison service (on the other) shall co-operate with one another with a view to improving the way in which those functions are exercised in relation to securing and maintaining the health of prisoners.

(2) The appropriate authority may by regulations make provision for or in connection with enabling prescribed NHS bodies (on the one hand) and the prison service (on the other) to enter into prescribed arrangements in relation to the exercise of –

(a) prescribed functions of the NHS bodies, and

(b) prescribed health-related functions of the prison service,

if the arrangements are likely to lead to an improvement in the way in which those functions are exercised in relation to securing and maintaining the health of prisoners.

(3) The arrangements which may be prescribed include arrangements –

(a) for or in connection with the establishment and maintenance of a fund –

(i) which is made up of contributions by one or more NHS bodies and by the prison service, and

(ii) out of which payments may be made towards expenditure incurred in the exercise of both prescribed functions of the NHS body or bodies and prescribed health-related functions of the prison service,

(b) for or in connection with the exercise by an NHS body on behalf of the prison service of prescribed health-related functions of the prison service in conjunction with the exercise by the NHS body of prescribed functions of theirs,

(c) for or in connection with the exercise by the prison service on behalf of an NHS body of prescribed functions of the NHS body in conjunction with the exercise by the prison service of prescribed health-related functions of the prison service,

    (d)   as to the provision of staff, goods, services or accommodation in connection with any arrangements mentioned in paragraph (a), (b) or (c),

    (e)   as to the making of payments by the prison service to an NHS body in connection with any arrangements mentioned in paragraph (b),

    (f)   as to the making of payments by an NHS body to the prison service in connection with any arrangements mentioned in paragraph (c).

(4)   Any arrangements made by virtue of this section do not affect the liability of NHS bodies, or of the prison service, for the exercise of any of their functions.

(5)   In this section –

    "appropriate authority" means –

        (a)   the Secretary of State, in relation to England, and

        (b)   the National Assembly for Wales, in relation to Wales,

    "NHS bodies" means Strategic Health Authorities, Primary Care Trusts, NHS trusts, Special Health Authorities, Health Authorities and Local Health Boards,

    "prison service" means the Minister of the Crown exercising functions in relation to prisons (within the meaning of the Prison Act 1952 (c. 52)),

    "Minister of the Crown" has the same meaning as in the Ministers of the Crown Act 1975 (c. 26).

24   Health and well-being strategies in Wales

(1)   It is the duty of –

    (a)   each local authority in Wales, and

    (b)   each Local Health Board any part of whose area lies within the area of the local authority,

jointly to formulate and implement a strategy for the health and well-being of members of the public in the local authority's area (a "health and well-being strategy").

(2)   The local authority and the Local Health Board (or Boards) responsible for a health and well-being strategy are referred to below as the "responsible bodies".

(3)   The responsible bodies are to have regard to their strategy in the exercise of their functions.

(4)   Each strategy is to be formulated in relation to a period of time to be specified in regulations to be made by the National Assembly for Wales.

(5)   The National Assembly for Wales may by regulations make further provision about health and well-being strategies.

(6)   The regulations may, in particular, make provision as to –

    (a)   the imposition of a duty on the responsible bodies to co-operate in formulating their strategy with prescribed persons or descriptions of person (including, for example, NHS trusts, Community Health Councils, voluntary bodies, and local businesses),

    (b)   steps which the responsible bodies must take before formulating the strategy,

    (c)   matters which the strategy must address,

    (d)   publication of the strategy,

(e) monitoring and review by the responsible bodies of the strategy and its implementation,

(f) the production of information and reports by the responsible bodies in relation to the strategy,

(g) the avoidance of duplication in the preparation of health and well-being strategies and other prescribed strategies or plans provided for under any other enactment.

(7) The National Assembly for Wales may –

(a) give directions to local authorities in Wales, Local Health Boards and NHS trusts in connection with health and well-being strategies,

(b) issue guidance to responsible bodies in connection with them.

(8) The power to give directions in subsection (7)(a) is without prejudice to any other power to give directions to the bodies mentioned there.

(9) In this section –

(a) "local authority" means county council or county borough council,

(b) "prescribed" means prescribed in regulations made by the National Assembly for Wales,

and references to NHS trusts are to be construed as references to NHS trusts all or most of whose hospitals, establishments and facilities are situated in Wales.

PART 2

HEALTH CARE PROFESSIONS

The Council for the Regulation of Health Care Professionals

25   The Council for the Regulation of Health Care Professionals

(1) There shall be a body corporate known as the Council for the Regulation of Health Care Professionals (in this group of sections referred to as "the Council").

(2) The general functions of the Council are –

(a) to promote the interests of patients and other members of the public in relation to the performance of their functions by the bodies mentioned in subsection (3) (in this group of sections referred to as "regulatory bodies"), and by their committees and officers,

(b) to promote best practice in the performance of those functions,

(c) to formulate principles relating to good professional self-regulation, and to encourage regulatory bodies to conform to them, and

(d) to promote co-operation between regulatory bodies; and between them, or any of them, and other bodies performing corresponding functions.

(3) The bodies referred to in subsection (2)(a) are –

(a) the General Medical Council,

(b) the General Dental Council,

(c) the General Optical Council,

(d) the General Osteopathic Council,

(e) the General Chiropractic Council,

   (f)   subject to section 26(5), the Royal Pharmaceutical Society of Great
          Britain,

   (g)   subject to section 26(6), the Pharmaceutical Society of Northern Ireland,

   (h)   until their abolition by virtue of section 60(3) of the 1999 Act –

          (i)   the United Kingdom Central Council for Nursing, Midwifery
                 and Health Visiting, and each of the National Boards for
                 Nursing, Midwifery and Health Visiting, and

          (ii)   the Council for Professions Supplementary to Medicine and
                 each Board established by or by virtue of the Professions
                 Supplementary to Medicine Act 1960 (c. 66),

   (i)   any regulatory body (within the meaning of Schedule 3 to the 1999 Act)
          established by an Order in Council under section 60 of that Act as the
          successor to a body mentioned in paragraph (h), and

   (j)   any other regulatory body (within that meaning) established by an
          Order in Council under that section.

(4)   Schedule 7 (which makes further provision about the Council) is to have effect.

(5)   "This group of sections" means this section and sections 26 to 29, and includes
      Schedule 7.

(6)   In this group of sections, references to regulation, in relation to a profession, are
      to be construed in accordance with paragraph 11(2) and (3) of Schedule 3 to the
      1999 Act.

26   Powers and duties of the Council: general

(1)   Except as mentioned in subsections (3) to (6), the Council may do anything
      which appears to it to be necessary or expedient for the purpose of, or in
      connection with, the performance of its functions.

(2)   The Council may, for example, do any of the following –

      (a)   investigate, and report on, the performance by each regulatory body of
             its functions,

      (b)   where a regulatory body performs functions corresponding to those of
             another body (including another regulatory body), investigate and
             report on how the performance of such functions by the bodies in
             question compares,

      (c)   recommend to a regulatory body changes to the way in which it
             performs any of its functions.

(3)   The Council may not do anything in relation to the case of any individual in
      relation to whom –

      (a)   there are, are to be, or have been proceedings before a committee of a
             regulatory body, or the regulatory body itself or any officer of the body,
             or

      (b)   an allegation has been made to the regulatory body, or one of its
             committees or officers, which could result in such proceedings.

(4)   Subsection (3) does not prevent the Council from taking action under section
      28 or 29, but action under section 29 may be taken only after the regulatory
      body's proceedings have ended.

(5) The Council may not do anything in relation to the functions of the Royal Pharmaceutical Society of Great Britain (or its Council, or an officer or committee of the Society) unless those functions are—

    (a) conferred on the Society (or its Council, or an officer or committee of the Society) by or by virtue of any provision of the Pharmacy Act 1954 (c. 61), other than section 17 (the benevolent fund),

    (b) conferred as mentioned in paragraph (a) by, or by virtue of, an Order in Council under section 60 of the 1999 Act, or

    (c) otherwise conferred as mentioned in paragraph (a) and relate to the regulation of the profession regulated by the Pharmacy Act 1954.

(6) The Council may not do anything in relation to the functions of the Pharmaceutical Society of Northern Ireland (or its Council, or an officer or committee of the Society) unless those functions are—

    (a) conferred on the Society (or its Council, or an officer or committee of the Society) by or by virtue of any provision of the Pharmacy (Northern Ireland) Order 1976 (S.I. 1976/1213 (N.I. 22)), other than Article 3(3)(e) (the benevolent functions),

    (b) conferred as mentioned in paragraph (a) by, or by virtue of, an Order in Council under section 60 of the 1999 Act or an order under section 56 of the Health and Personal Social Services Act (Northern Ireland) 2001 (c. 3) (which makes provision corresponding to section 60 of the 1999 Act), or

    (c) otherwise conferred as mentioned in paragraph (a) and relate to the regulation of the profession regulated by the Pharmacy (Northern Ireland) Order 1976.

(7) The Secretary of State, the National Assembly for Wales, the Scottish Ministers or the Department of Health, Social Services and Public Safety in Northern Ireland may ask the Council for advice on any matter connected with a profession appearing to him or them to be a health care profession.

(8) The Council must comply with such a request.

(9) In section 60(1) of the 1999 Act (regulation of health care and associated professions), after paragraph (b) there is inserted—

    "(c) modifying the functions, powers or duties of the Council for the Regulation of Health Care Professionals,

    (d) modifying the list of regulatory bodies (in section 25(3) of the National Health Service Reform and Health Care Professions Act 2002) in relation to which that Council performs its functions,

    (e) modifying, as respects any such regulatory body, the range of functions of that body in relation to which the Council performs its functions."

(10) In Schedule 3 to the 1999 Act (which makes further provision about orders under section 60 of that Act), in paragraph 7, after sub-paragraph (3) there is inserted—

    "(4) An Order may not confer any additional powers of direction over the Council for the Regulation of Health Care Professionals."

(11) In subsections (3) and (4), "proceedings", in relation to a regulatory body, or one of its committees or officers, includes a process of decision-making by

which a decision could be made affecting the registration of the individual in question.

(12)   In this section, "health care profession" means a profession (whether or not regulated by or by virtue of any enactment) which is concerned (wholly or partly) with the physical or mental health of individuals.

27   Regulatory bodies and the Council

(1)   Each regulatory body must in the exercise of its functions co-operate with the Council.

(2)   If the Council considers that it would be desirable to do so for the protection of members of the public, it may give directions requiring a regulatory body to make rules (under any power the body has to do so) to achieve an effect which must be specified in the directions.

(3)   The Council may give such directions only in relation to rules which must be approved by the Privy Council (whether by order or not) or by the Department of Health, Social Services and Public Safety in Northern Ireland before coming into force.

(4)   The Council must send a copy of any such directions to the relevant authority.

(5)   The relevant authority is the Secretary of State or, if the regulatory body in question is the Pharmaceutical Society of Northern Ireland, the Department of Health, Social Services and Public Safety there.

(6)   The directions do not come into force until the date specified in an order made by the relevant authority.

(7)   The Secretary of State must lay before both Houses of Parliament, or (as the case may be) the Department of Health, Social Services and Public Safety must lay before the Northern Ireland Assembly, a draft of an order —
    (a)   setting out any directions he or it receives pursuant to subsection (4), and
    (b)   specifying the date on which the directions are to come into force.

(8)   Subsections (4) to (7) apply also to —
    (a)   directions varying earlier directions, and
    (b)   directions revoking earlier directions, and given after —
        (i)   both Houses of Parliament have resolved to approve the draft order specifying the date on which the earlier directions are to come into force, or (as the case may be)
        (ii)   the Northern Ireland Assembly has done so.

(9)   Subsections (4) and (5) apply also to directions —
    (a)   revoking earlier directions, but
    (b)   which do not fall within subsection (8)(b),
    but subsections (6) and (7) do not apply to such directions.

(10)   If the Council gives directions which fall within subsection (9), the earlier directions which those directions revoke shall be treated as if subsections (6) and (7) had never applied to them, and as never in force.

(11)   A regulatory body must comply with directions given under subsection (2) which have come into force and have not been revoked.

(12) A regulatory body is not to be taken to have failed to comply with such directions merely because a court determines that the rules made pursuant to the directions are to be construed in such a way that the effect referred to in subsection (2) is not achieved.

(13) The Secretary of State shall make provision in regulations as to the procedure to be followed in relation to the giving of directions under subsection (2).

(14) The regulations must, in particular, make provision requiring the Council to consult a regulatory body before giving directions relating to it under subsection (2).

(15) In this section –
   (a) "making" rules includes amending or revoking rules, and
   (b) "rules" includes regulations, byelaws and schemes.

28 Complaints about regulatory bodies

(1) The Secretary of State may make provision in regulations about the investigation by the Council of complaints made to it about the way in which a regulatory body has exercised any of its functions.

(2) The regulations may, in particular, make provision as to –
   (a) who (or what description of person) is entitled to complain,
   (b) the nature of complaints which the Council must (or need not) investigate,
   (c) matters which are excluded from investigation,
   (d) requirements to be complied with by a person who makes a complaint,
   (e) the procedure to be followed by the Council in investigating complaints,
   (f) the making of recommendations or reports by the Council following investigations,
   (g) the confidentiality, or disclosure, of any information supplied to the Council or acquired by it in connection with an investigation,
   (h) the use which the Council may make of any such information,
   (i) the making of payments to any persons in connection with investigations,
   (j) privilege in relation to any matter published by the Council in the exercise of its functions under the regulations.

(3) The regulations may also make provision –
   (a) empowering the Council to require persons to attend before it,
   (b) empowering the Council to require persons to give evidence or produce documents to it,
   (c) about the admissibility of evidence,
   (d) enabling the Council to administer oaths.

(4) No person shall be required by or by virtue of regulations under this section to give any evidence or produce any document or other material to the Council which he could not be compelled to give or produce in civil proceedings before the High Court or, in Scotland, the Court of Session.

29   Reference of disciplinary cases by Council to court

(1)   This section applies to —

       (a)   a direction of the Statutory Committee of the Royal Pharmaceutical Society of Great Britain under section 8 of the Pharmacy Act 1954 (c. 61) (control of registrations by Statutory Committee) or section 80 of the Medicines Act 1968 (c. 67) (power to disqualify and direct removal from register),

       (b)   a direction of the Statutory Committee of the Pharmaceutical Society of Northern Ireland under Article 20 of the Pharmacy (Northern Ireland) Order 1976 (S.I. 1976/1213 (N.I. 22)) (control of registrations by Statutory Committee) or section 80 of the Medicines Act 1968,

       (c)   a direction by the Professional Conduct Committee of the General Medical Council under section 36 of the Medical Act 1983 (c. 54) (professional misconduct and related offences),

       (d)   a direction by the Committee on Professional Performance of the General Medical Council under section 36A of that Act (professional performance),

       (e)   a determination by the Professional Conduct Committee of the General Dental Council under section 27 of the Dentists Act 1984 (c. 24) (erasure or suspension of registration for crime or misconduct),

       (f)   a disciplinary order made by the Disciplinary Committee of the General Optical Council under section 17 of the Opticians Act 1989 (c. 44) (powers of Disciplinary Committee),

       (g)   any step taken by the Professional Conduct Committee of the General Osteopathic Council under section 22 of the Osteopaths Act 1993 (c. 21) (which relates to action to be taken in cases of allegations referred to the Professional Conduct Committee),

       (h)   any step taken by the Professional Conduct Committee of the General Chiropractic Council under section 22 of the Chiropractors Act 1994 (c. 17) (which relates to corresponding matters),

       (i)   any corresponding measure taken in relation to a nurse, midwife or health visitor,

       (j)   any corresponding measure taken in relation to a member of a profession regulated by the Professions Supplementary to Medicine Act 1960 (c. 66) or, after the repeal of that Act by virtue of section 60(3) of the 1999 Act, by any such Order in Council under section 60 of the 1999 Act as is mentioned in section 25(3)(i).

(2)   This section also applies to —

       (a)   a final decision of the relevant committee not to take any disciplinary measure under the provision referred to in whichever of paragraphs (a) to (h) of subsection (1) applies,

       (b)   any corresponding decision taken in relation to a nurse, midwife or health visitor, or to any such person as is mentioned in subsection (1)(j) and

       (c)   a decision of the relevant regulatory body, or one of its committees or officers, to restore a person to the register following his removal from it in accordance with any of the measures referred to in paragraphs (a) to (j) of subsection (1).

(3)   The things to which this section applies are referred to below as "relevant decisions".

(4)   If the Council considers that—

    (a)   a relevant decision falling within subsection (1) has been unduly lenient, whether as to any finding of professional misconduct or fitness to practise on the part of the practitioner concerned (or lack of such a finding), or as to any penalty imposed, or both, or

    (b)   a relevant decision falling within subsection (2) should not have been made,

and that it would be desirable for the protection of members of the public for the Council to take action under this section, the Council may refer the case to the relevant court.

(5)   In subsection (4), the "relevant court"—

    (a)   in the case of a person whose address in the register of practitioners in question is (or if he were registered would be) in Scotland, means the Court of Session,

    (b)   in the case of a person whose address in the register of practitioners in question is (or if he were registered would be) in Northern Ireland, means the High Court of Justice in Northern Ireland, and

    (c)   in the case of any other person (including one who is not registered and is not seeking registration or restoration to the register), means the High Court of Justice in England and Wales.

(6)   The Council may not so refer a case after the end of the period of four weeks beginning with the last date on which the practitioner concerned has the right to appeal against the relevant decision.

(7)   If the Council does so refer a case—

    (a)   the case is to be treated by the court to which it has been referred as an appeal by the Council against the relevant decision (even though the Council was not a party to the proceedings resulting in the relevant decision), and

    (b)   the body which made the relevant decision is to be a respondent.

(8)   The court may—

    (a)   dismiss the appeal,

    (b)   allow the appeal and quash the relevant decision,

    (c)   substitute for the relevant decision any other decision which could have been made by the committee or other person concerned, or

    (d)   remit the case to the committee or other person concerned to dispose of the case in accordance with the directions of the court,

and may make such order as to costs (or, in Scotland, expenses) as it thinks fit.

Appeals

30   Medical practitioners

(1)   The Medical Act 1983 (c. 54) is amended as follows.

(2)   In section 40 (appeals)—

    (a)   in subsection (1), paragraph (c) is omitted,

    (b)   after subsection (1), there is inserted—

"(1A)   A decision of the General Council under section 39 above giving a direction for erasure is also an appealable decision for the purposes of this section.",

(c)   for subsection (3) there is substituted –

"(3)   A person in respect of whom an appealable decision falling within subsection (1) has been taken may, before the end of the period of 28 days beginning with the date on which notification of the decision was served under section 36(6), 36A(7), or 37(6) above, or section 41(7) or 45(7) below, appeal against the decision to the relevant court.

(3A)   In subsection (3), "the relevant court" –

     (a)   in the case of a person whose address in the register is (or if he were registered would be) in Scotland, means the Court of Session,

     (b)   in the case of a person whose address in the register is (or if he were registered would be) in Northern Ireland, means the High Court of Justice in Northern Ireland, and

     (c)   in the case of any other person (including one appealing against a decision falling within subsection (1)(e)), means the High Court of Justice in England and Wales.

(3B)   A person in respect of whom an appealable decision falling within subsection (1A) above has been taken may, before the end of the period of 28 days beginning with the date on which notification of the decision was served under section 39(2), appeal against the decision to a county court or, in Scotland, the sheriff in whose sheriffdom the address in the register is situated.",

(d)   subsections (4) to (6), (9) and (10) are omitted, and

(e)   for subsections (7) and (8) there is substituted –

"(7)   On an appeal under this section from the Professional Conduct Committee, the Committee on Professional Performance or the Health Committee, the court may –

     (a)   dismiss the appeal,

     (b)   allow the appeal and quash the direction or variation appealed against,

     (c)   substitute for the direction or variation appealed against any other direction or variation which could have been given or made by the committee concerned, or

     (d)   remit the case to the committee concerned to dispose of the case in accordance with the directions of the court,

and may make such order as to costs (or, in Scotland, expenses) as it thinks fit.

(8)   On an appeal under this section from the General Council, the court (or the sheriff) may –

     (a)   dismiss the appeal,

     (b)   allow the appeal and quash the direction appealed against, or

(c) remit the case to the General Council to dispose of the case in accordance with the directions of the court (or the sheriff),

and may make such order as to costs (or in Scotland, expenses) as it (or he) thinks fit."

(3) In Schedule 4 (proceedings before Professional Conduct, Health and Preliminary Proceedings Committees) —

(a) in paragraph 3(b), the words "to Her Majesty in Council" are omitted and for "the Judicial Committee" there is substituted "the court (or the sheriff)",

(b) in paragraph 10(1) —

(i) for "section 37 of this Act and" there is substituted "section 37 of this Act,",

(ii) after "or 37 of this Act", there is inserted "and a direction for erasure given by the General Council under section 39 of this Act", and

(iii) in paragraph (a), for the words "mentioned in subsection (3) of that section" there is substituted "specified in that section",

(c) paragraph 10(2) is omitted, and

(d) in paragraph 10(3) —

(i) "or (2)" is omitted,

(ii) "or that sub-paragraph as applied by sub-paragraph (2) above" is omitted,

(iii) for "mentioned in section 40(3)" there is substituted "specified in section 40", and

(iv) for "mentioned in the said section 40(3)" there is substituted "specified in section 40 of this Act".

31 Dentists

(1) The Dentists Act 1984 (c. 24) is amended as follows.

(2) In section 29 (appeals) —

(a) in subsection (1), for the words from "to Her" to the end there is substituted "against that determination or direction to the relevant court.",

(b) after subsection (1) there is inserted —

"(1A) In subsection (1), "the relevant court" —

(a) in the case of a person whose address in the register is (or if he were registered would be) in Scotland, means the Court of Session,

(b) in the case of a person whose address in the register is (or if he were registered would be) in Northern Ireland, means the High Court of Justice in Northern Ireland, and

(c) in the case of any other person, means the High Court of Justice in England and Wales.",

(c) subsection (2) is omitted, and

(d) for subsection (3) there is substituted —

"(3) On an appeal under this section, the court may —

(a)   dismiss the appeal,

(b)   allow the appeal and quash the determination or direction appealed against,

(c)   (in the case of an appeal against a determination under section 27 above or a direction under section 28 above) substitute for the determination or direction appealed against any other determination or direction which could have been made or given by the Professional Conduct Committee or (as the case may be) the Health Committee, or

(d)   remit the case to the Professional Conduct Committee, the Health Committee or the Continuing Professional Development Committee to dispose of the case under section 27 or 28 above or Schedule 3A to this Act in accordance with the directions of the court,

and may make such order as to costs (or, in Scotland, expenses) as it thinks fit."

(3)   In section 44 (withdrawal of privilege from body corporate) –

     (a)   in subsection (4) –

         (i)   after "days" there is inserted "from service", and

         (ii)   for the words from "in accordance" to "Majesty in Council" there is substituted "appeal to the relevant court", and

     (b)   after subsection (4) there is inserted –

     "(4A)   In subsection (4), "the relevant court" –

         (a)   where the registered office of the body corporate is in Northern Ireland, means the High Court of Justice in Northern Ireland,

         (b)   where the registered office of the body corporate is in Scotland, means the Court of Session,

         (c)   where the registered office of the body corporate is in any other place, means the High Court of Justice in England and Wales."

(4)   In section 51, the words from "(other" to "appeals)" are omitted.

(5)   In section 34A (professional training and development requirements), in subsection (7)(b), for "to Her Majesty in Council" there is substituted "under section 29 above to the relevant court".

(6)   Subsection (5) has effect –

     (a)   upon the coming into force of this section, if that happens after the coming into force of article 8 of the Dentists Act 1984 (Amendment) Order 2001 (S.I. 2001/3926) ("the Dentists Order") so far as that article effects the insertion into the Dentists Act 1984 (c. 24) of the new section 34A(7)(b),

     (b)   otherwise, immediately after the coming into force to that extent of that article.

(7)   If this section comes into force before article 10(3) of the Dentists Order –

     (a)   paragraphs (b), (c) and (d) of article 10(3) of that Order are revoked upon the coming into force of this section, and

     (b)   until the coming into force of the remainder of article 10(3) of that Order, section 29 of the Dentists Act 1984 (c. 24) (as amended by this section) is to be read with the modifications set out in subsection (8).

(8)   The modifications are that section 29 is to be read as if —

     (a)   in each of paragraphs (a) and (b) of subsection (1A), the words "(or if he were registered would be)" were omitted,

     (b)   in paragraph (c) of subsection (3), the words "(in the case of an appeal against a determination under section 27 above or a direction under section 28 above)" were omitted, and

     (c)   in paragraph (d) of subsection (3) —

         (i)   for the words ", the Health Committee or the Continuing Professional Development Committee" there were substituted "or the Health Committee", and

         (ii)   the words "or Schedule 3A to this Act" were omitted.

32   Opticians

(1)   Section 23 of the Opticians Act 1989 (c. 44) (appeals in disciplinary and other cases) is amended as follows.

(2)   For subsection (1) there is substituted —

    "(1)   An individual or body corporate who is notified under subsection (11) of section 17 —

     (a)   that a disciplinary order has been made against him under that section; or

     (b)   that a direction has been given in respect of him under subsection (9) of that section,

    may, before the end of the period of 28 days beginning with the date on which notification was served, appeal against that order or direction to the relevant court.

    (1A)   In subsection (1), "the relevant court" —

     (a)   in the case of an individual whose address in the register is in Scotland, or a body corporate whose registered office is in Scotland, means the Court of Session,

     (b)   in the case of an individual whose address in the register is in Northern Ireland, or a body corporate whose registered office is in Northern Ireland, means the High Court of Justice in Northern Ireland, and

     (c)   in the case of any other individual or body corporate, means the High Court of Justice in England and Wales.

    (1B)   An individual or body corporate who is notified under subsection (3) of section 19 above that a direction has been given in respect of him under that section may, before the end of the period of 28 days beginning with the date on which notification was served, appeal against that direction to a county court or, in Scotland, the sheriff in whose sheriffdom the address in the register or (as the case may be) the registered office is situated.

    (1C)   On an appeal under this section, the court (or the sheriff) may —

     (a)   dismiss the appeal,

     (b)   allow the appeal and quash the order or direction appealed against,

     (c)   substitute for the order or direction appealed against any other order or direction which could have been made by the Disciplinary Committee, or

     (d)   remit the case to the Disciplinary Committee to dispose of the case in accordance with the directions of the court (or the sheriff),

and may make such order as to costs (or, in Scotland, expenses) as it (or he) thinks fit."

(3)   In subsection (2), for "any such appeal", where it first appears, there is substituted "any appeal under this section".

33   Osteopaths

(1)   The Osteopaths Act 1993 (c. 21) is amended as follows.

(2)   In section 10 (fraud or error in relation to registration) –

     (a)   in subsection (7), for "Her Majesty in Council" there is substituted "a county court or, in the case of a person whose address in the register is in Scotland, the sheriff in whose sheriffdom the address is situated",

     (b)   for subsection (8) there is substituted –

       "(8)   Any such appeal must be brought before the end of the period of 28 days beginning with the date on which notification of the order was served under subsection (6).",

     (c)   subsection (10) is omitted, and

     (d)   for subsection (11) there is substituted –

       "(11)   On an appeal under this section, the court (or the sheriff) may –

          (a)   dismiss the appeal,

          (b)   allow the appeal and quash the order appealed against, or

          (c)   remit the case to the General Council to dispose of the case in accordance with the directions of the court (or the sheriff),

        and may make such order as to costs (or, in Scotland, expenses) as it (or he) thinks fit."

(3)   In section 22 (consideration of allegations by the Professional Conduct Committee), in each of subsections (6) and (8), for "recommendation under section 31(8)(c)" there is substituted "decision of a court on an appeal under section 31".

(4)   In section 23 (consideration of allegations by the Health Committee), in each of subsections (4), (5) and (6), for "recommendation under section 31(8)(c)" there is substituted "decision of a court on an appeal under section 31".

(5)   In section 29 (appeals against decisions of the Registrar), for subsections (4) to (6) there is substituted –

       "(4)   A person aggrieved by the decision of the General Council on an appeal under this section may appeal to a county court or, in the case of a person whose address in the register is (or if he were registered would be) in Scotland, the sheriff in whose sheriffdom the address is situated.

(4A) On an appeal under subsection (4) above, the court (or the sheriff) may —

    (a) dismiss the appeal,

    (b) allow the appeal and quash the decision appealed against,

    (c) substitute for the decision appealed against any other decision which could have been made by the Registrar, or

    (d) remit the case to the General Council to dispose of the case in accordance with the directions of the court (or the sheriff),

and may make such order as to costs (or, in Scotland, expenses) as it (or he) thinks fit."

(6) In section 31 (appeals against decisions of the Professional Conduct Committee and appeal tribunals) —

    (a) in subsection (1), for the words from "sent to him" to the end there is substituted "served on him, appeal against it to the relevant court.",

    (b) after subsection (1) there is inserted —

"(1A) In subsection (1), "the relevant court" —

    (a) in the case of a person whose address in the register is (or if he were registered would be) in Scotland, means the Court of Session,

    (b) in the case of a person whose address in the register is (or if he were registered would be) in Northern Ireland, means the High Court of Justice in Northern Ireland, and

    (c) in the case of any other person, means the High Court of Justice in England and Wales.",

    (c) subsections (3) to (5) and (7) are omitted, and

    (d) for subsection (8) there is substituted —

"(8) On an appeal under this section, the court may —

    (a) dismiss the appeal,

    (b) allow the appeal and quash the decision appealed against,

    (c) substitute for the decision appealed against any other decision which could have been made by the Professional Conduct Committee or (as the case may be) Health Committee, or

    (d) remit the case to the Committee or appeal tribunal concerned to dispose of the case in accordance with the directions of the court,

and may make such order as to costs (or, in Scotland, expenses) as it thinks fit."

(7) In section 35 (rules), subsection (3) is omitted.

34 Chiropractors

(1) The Chiropractors Act 1994 (c. 17) is amended as follows.

(2) In section 10 (fraud or error in relation to registration) —

    (a) in subsection (7), for "Her Majesty in Council" there is substituted "a county court or, in the case of a person whose address in the register is in Scotland, the sheriff in whose sheriffdom the address is situated",

      (b)   for subsection (8) there is substituted —

          "(8)   Any such appeal must be brought before the end of the period of 28 days beginning with the date on which notification of the order was served under subsection (6).",

      (c)   subsection (10) is omitted, and

      (d)   for subsection (11) there is substituted —

          "(11)   On an appeal under this section, the court (or the sheriff) may —

             (a)   dismiss the appeal,

             (b)   allow the appeal and quash the order appealed against, or

             (c)   remit the case to the General Council to dispose of the case in accordance with the directions of the court (or the sheriff),

          and may make such order as to costs (or, in Scotland, expenses) as it (or he) thinks fit."

  (3)   In section 22 (consideration of allegations by the Professional Conduct Committee), in each of subsections (7) and (9), for "recommendation under section 31(8)(c)" there is substituted "decision of a court on an appeal under section 31".

  (4)   In section 23 (consideration of allegations by the Health Committee), in each of subsections (4), (5) and (6), for "recommendation under section 31(8)(c)" there is substituted "decision of a court on an appeal under section 31".

  (5)   In section 29 (appeals against decisions of the Registrar), for subsections (4) to (6) there is substituted —

          "(4)   A person aggrieved by the decision of the General Council on an appeal under this section may appeal to a county court or, in the case of a person whose address in the register is (or if he were registered would be) in Scotland, the sheriff in whose sheriffdom the address is situated.

          (4A)   On an appeal under subsection (4) above, the court (or the sheriff) may —

             (a)   dismiss the appeal,

             (b)   allow the appeal and quash the decision appealed against,

             (c)   substitute for the decision appealed against any other decision which could have been made by the Registrar, or

             (d)   remit the case to the General Council to dispose of the case in accordance with the directions of the court (or the sheriff),

          and may make such order as to costs (or, in Scotland, expenses) as it (or he) thinks fit."

  (6)   In section 31 (appeals against decisions of the Professional Conduct Committee and appeal tribunals) —

      (a)   in subsection (1), for the words from "sent to him" to the end there is substituted "served on him, appeal against it to the relevant court.",

      (b)   after subsection (1) there is inserted —

          "(1A)   In subsection (1), "the relevant court" —

             (a)   in the case of a person whose address in the register is (or if he were registered would be) in Scotland, means the Court of Session,

> > (b) in the case of a person whose address in the register is (or if he were registered would be) in Northern Ireland, means the High Court of Justice in Northern Ireland, and
> >
> > (c) in the case of any other person, means the High Court of Justice in England and Wales.",
>
> (c) subsections (3) to (5) and (7) are omitted, and
>
> (d) for subsection (8) there is substituted —
>
> > "(8) On an appeal under this section, the court may —
> >
> > > (a) dismiss the appeal,
> > >
> > > (b) allow the appeal and quash the decision appealed against,
> > >
> > > (c) substitute for the decision appealed against any other decision which could have been made by the Professional Conduct Committee or (as the case may be) Health Committee, or
> > >
> > > (d) remit the case to the Committee or appeal tribunal concerned to dispose of the case in accordance with the directions of the court,
> >
> > and may make such order as to costs (or, in Scotland, expenses) as it thinks fit."

(7) In section 35 (rules), subsection (3) is omitted.

The pharmacy profession

35 Regulation of the profession of pharmacy

In Schedule 3 to the 1999 Act (which makes provision in relation to orders under section 60 of that Act regulating health care and associated professions), in paragraph 2, for sub-paragraphs (2) and (3) there is substituted —

> "(2) But (subject to paragraph 12) an order may not amend the Medicines Act 1968 except in connection with the regulation of the profession regulated by the Pharmacy Act 1954."

PART 3

MISCELLANEOUS

36 Amendments of health service legislation in connection with consolidation

(1) The Secretary of State may by order make such amendments of the legislation relating to the health service in England and Wales as in his opinion facilitate, or are otherwise desirable in connection with, the consolidation of the whole or greater part of that legislation.

(2) An order under this section shall not come into force unless —

> (a) a single Act, or
>
> (b) a group of two or more Acts,

is passed consolidating the whole or greater part of the legislation relating to the health service in England and Wales (with or without other legislation relating to any of the health services).

(3) If such an Act or group of Acts is passed, the order shall (by virtue of this subsection) come into force immediately before the Act or group of Acts comes into force.

(4) Once an order under this section has come into force, no further order may be made under this section.

(5) In this section —

"the health services" means any of the health services within the meaning of the 1977 Act, the National Health Service (Scotland) Act 1978 (c. 29) or the Health and Personal Social Services (Northern Ireland) Order 1972 (S.I. 1972/1265 (N.I. 14)),

"the legislation relating to the health service in England and Wales" means the 1977 Act and any other Act relating to the health service (within the meaning of that Act), whenever passed.

37   Minor and consequential amendments and repeals

(1) The minor and consequential amendments specified in Schedule 8 are to have effect.

(2) The enactments specified in Schedule 9 are repealed to the extent specified.

38   Regulations and orders

(1) Any power under this Act to make any order or regulations is (except in the case of orders under section 22(5)) exercisable by statutory instrument or, in the case of an order made by the Department of Health, Social Services and Public Safety in Northern Ireland under section 27, by statutory rule for the purposes of the Statutory Rules (Northern Ireland) Order 1979 (S.I. 1979/1573 (N.I. 12)).

(2) A statutory instrument containing any order or regulations made by the Secretary of State under this Act, other than regulations under section 28 or an order under section 27, 36 or 42(3), shall be subject to annulment in pursuance of a resolution of either House of Parliament.

(3) A statutory instrument containing regulations under section 28 or an order under section 36, or an order of the Secretary of State under section 27, shall not be made unless a draft of the instrument has been laid before, and approved by a resolution of, each House of Parliament.

(4) No order shall be made by the Department of Health, Social Services and Public Safety in Northern Ireland under section 27 unless a draft of the order has been laid before, and approved by resolution of, the Northern Ireland Assembly.

(5) Any power under this Act to make any order or regulations may be exercised —

    (a) either in relation to all cases to which the power extends, or in relation to those cases subject to specified exceptions, or in relation to any specified cases or classes of case,

    (b) so as to make, as respects the cases in relation to which it is exercised —

       (i) the full provision to which the power extends or any less provision (whether by way of exception or otherwise),

       (ii) the same provision for all cases in relation to which the power is exercised, or different provision for different cases or different classes of case or different provision as respects the same case or class of case for different purposes of this Act,

    (iii)   any such provision either unconditionally or subject to any specified condition.

(6)   Where any such power is expressed to be exercisable for alternative purposes it may be exercised in relation to the same case for any or all of those purposes.

(7)   Any such power includes power—

    (a)   to make such incidental, supplementary, consequential, saving or transitional provision (including provision amending, repealing or revoking enactments) as the authority making the order or regulations considers to be expedient, and

    (b)   to provide for a person to exercise a discretion in dealing with any matter.

(8)   Subsections (5) to (7) do not apply to orders under section 27.

(9)   Subject to subsection (8), nothing in this Act shall be read as affecting the generality of subsection (7).

(10)   Directions given in pursuance of any provision of this Act are, except where otherwise stated, to be given by instrument in writing.

(11)   Any power conferred by this Act to give directions by instrument in writing includes power to vary or revoke them by subsequent directions.

39   Supplementary and consequential provision etc

(1)   The Secretary of State may by regulations make—

    (a)   such supplementary, incidental or consequential provision, or

    (b)   such transitory, transitional or saving provision,

as he considers necessary or expedient for the purposes of, or in consequence of or for giving full effect to any provision of this Act.

(2)   The provision which may be made under subsection (1) includes provision amending or repealing any enactment, instrument or document, including an enactment contained in an Act passed in the same session as this Act.

(3)   The power to make regulations under this section is also exercisable by the National Assembly for Wales, in relation to provision dealing with matters with respect to which functions are exercisable by the Assembly.

(4)   Nothing in this Act shall be read as affecting the generality of subsection (1).

40   Wales

(1)   In Schedule 1 to the National Assembly for Wales (Transfer of Functions) Order 1999 (S.I. 1999/672), any reference to an Act which is amended by this Act is (as from the time when the Act is so amended) to be treated as referring to the Act as so amended.

(2)   Subsection (1) does not affect the power to make further Orders varying or omitting any such reference.

41   Financial provisions

There shall be paid out of money provided by Parliament−

(a)   any expenditure incurred by the Secretary of State in consequence of this Act, and

(b)   any increase attributable to this Act in the sums payable out of money so provided by virtue of any other Act.

42   Short title, interpretation, commencement and extent

(1)   This Act may be cited as the National Health Service Reform and Health Care Professions Act 2002.

(2)   In this Act−

"the 1977 Act" means the National Health Service Act 1977 (c. 49),

"the 1999 Act" means the Health Act 1999 (c. 8),

"NHS trust" has the same meaning as in the 1977 Act.

(3)   This Act, apart from−

(a)   this section and sections 38 to 41, and

(b)   any other provision of this Act so far as it confers any power to make an order or regulations under this Act,

shall come into force on such day as the appropriate authority may by order appoint, and different days may be appointed for different provisions and for different purposes.

(4)   In subsection (3), the "appropriate authority" is−

(a)   in relation to sections 1 to 5, 7, 8, 15 to 22, Part 2, and section 36, the Secretary of State,

(b)   in relation to sections 11 to 14, the Secretary of State after consulting the National Assembly for Wales,

(c)   in relation to sections 6, 9 and 24, the National Assembly for Wales,

(d)   in relation to sections 10 and 23−

(i)   the Secretary of State, in relation to England, and

(ii)   the National Assembly for Wales, in relation to Wales,

(e)   in relation to section 37−

(i)   the Secretary of State, as respects any amendment or repeal consequential on provisions falling within paragraph (a),

(ii)   the Secretary of State, after consulting the National Assembly for Wales, as respects any amendment or repeal consequential on provisions falling within paragraph (b),

(iii)   the National Assembly for Wales, as respects any amendment or repeal consequential on provisions falling within paragraph (c),

(iv)   otherwise, the Secretary of State, in relation to England, and the National Assembly for Wales, in relation to Wales.

(5)   Subject to subsection (6), this Act extends to the whole of the United Kingdom, except for Part 1, which extends to England and Wales only.

(6)   The extent of any amendment or repeal made by this Act is the same as that of the enactment amended or repealed.

(7) Subsection (6) does not apply to the amendment of the Police Act 1997 (c. 50) made by paragraph 64 of Schedule 2, which extends to England and Wales only.

(8) The Secretary of State may by order provide that so much of this Act as extends to England and Wales is to apply to the Isles of Scilly with such modifications (if any) as are specified in the order; but otherwise this Act does not extend there.

SCHEDULES

SCHEDULE 1   Section 1(3)

ENGLISH HEALTH AUTHORITIES: CHANGE OF NAME

PART 1

AMENDMENTS OF 1977 ACT

1   The 1977 Act is amended as follows.

2   In section 12 (provision supplementary to sections 8 and 11), in subsection (2)(a), at the beginning there is inserted "Strategic Health Authorities and".

3   In section 16 (exercise of functions) —
  (a) in subsection (1), after "exercisable by" there is inserted "a Strategic Health Authority or",
  (b) in subsection (2) —
   (i) before paragraph (a) there is inserted —
     "(za)   by another Strategic Health Authority;", and
   (ii) in paragraph (c), after "Local Health Boards" (inserted by paragraph 5 of Schedule 5) there is inserted ", other Strategic Health Authorities", and
  (c) in subsection (4)(a), before "Health Authority" (in both places) there is inserted "Strategic Health Authority or".

4   In section 16B (exercise of functions by Primary Care Trusts) —
  (a) in subsection (2)(c), after "following:" there is inserted "Strategic Health Authorities,", and
  (b) in subsection (3)(c), after "one or more" there is inserted "Strategic Health Authorities,".

5   In section 16C (advice for Health Authorities and Primary Care Trusts) —
  (a) in subsection (1), after "Every" there is inserted "Strategic Health Authority and every", and
  (b) in subsection (2), before "Health Authorities" there is inserted "Strategic Health Authorities and".

6   In section 16D (Secretary of State's directions: distribution of functions) —
  (a) in subsection (1), after "direct a" there is inserted "Strategic Health Authority,", and
  (b) in subsection (2), after "of a" there is inserted "Strategic Health Authority or".

7   In section 17 (Secretary of State's directions: exercise of functions), in subsection (2), before paragraph (a) there is inserted —

National Health Service Reform and Health Care Professions Act 2002 (c. 17)
Schedule 1 – English Health Authorities: change of name
Part 1 – Amendments of 1977 Act

51

"(za) Strategic Health Authorities;".

8   In section 17B (Health Authority's directions: exercise of functions), in subsection (1), for "Health Authority" there is substituted "Strategic Health Authority".

9   In section 18 (directions and regulations under preceding provisions), in subsection (1B), for "Health Authority" there is substituted "Strategic Health Authority".

10   In section 22 (co-operation between Health Authorities and local authorities), in subsection (1A), before paragraph (a) there is inserted –
         "(za) a Strategic Health Authority;".

11   In section 23 (voluntary organisations and other bodies), in subsection (2), after "or by a" there is inserted "Strategic Health Authority,".

12   In section 26 (supply of goods and services by the Secretary of State) –
         (a)   in subsection (1)(b), after "State or by a" there is inserted "Strategic Health Authority,",
         (b)   in subsection (3), in each of paragraphs (b) and (c), after "or a" there is inserted "Strategic Health Authority,", and
         (c)   in subsection (4)(b), after "providing" there is inserted "Strategic Health Authorities,".

13   In section 27 (conditions of supply under section 26) –
         (a)   in subsection (1) –
               (i)   after "officer of a" there is inserted "Strategic Health Authority,", and
               (ii)   after "that the" there is inserted "Strategic Health Authority,", and
         (b)   in subsection (3), after "directions to" there is inserted "Strategic Health Authorities,".

14   In section 28 (supply of goods and services by local authorities) –
         (a)   in subsection (1), after "any" there is inserted "Strategic Health Authority,", and
         (b)   in subsection (3) –
               (i)   after "available to" there is inserted "Strategic Health Authorities,", and
               (ii)   after "to enable" there is inserted "Strategic Health Authorities,".

15   In section 28A (power to make payments towards expenditure on community services), in subsection (2B), after "by a" there is inserted "Strategic Health Authority,".

16   In section 28BB (power of local authorities to make payments to NHS bodies), in subsection (2), after "means a" there is inserted "Strategic Health Authority or".

17   In section 37 (Dental Practice Board), in subsection (1)(b), for "Health Authority" there is substituted "Strategic Health Authority".

18   In section 49S (the Family Health Services Appeal Authority), in subsection (8)(b), after "by a" there is inserted "Strategic Health Authority,".

52   *National Health Service Reform and Health Care Professions Act 2002 (c. 17)*
Schedule 1 – English Health Authorities: change of name
Part 1 – Amendments of 1977 Act

19   In section 51 (university clinical teaching and research) –

    (a)   in subsection (2) –

        (i)   after "by a" there is inserted "Strategic Health Authority,", and

        (ii)   after "by the" there is inserted "Strategic Health Authority,", and

    (b)   in subsection (3), before paragraph (a) there is inserted –

        "(za)   Strategic Health Authorities;".

20   In section 65 (accommodation and services for private patients), before "Health Authority or", in each place where it occurs, there is inserted "Strategic Health Authority,".

21   In section 84A (intervention orders), in subsection (2), before paragraph (a) there is inserted –

        "(za)   Strategic Health Authorities,".

22   In section 84B (intervention orders: effect) –

    (a)   in subsection (1), in each of paragraphs (a) and (b), after "of a" there is inserted "Strategic Health Authority,", and

    (b)   in subsection (6), before "a Health Authority" there is inserted "a Strategic Health Authority or".

23   In section 85 (default powers), in subsection (1), before paragraph (a) there is inserted –

        "(za)   a Strategic Health Authority;".

24   In section 90 (gifts on trust), after "A" there is inserted "Strategic Health Authority,".

25   In section 91 (private trusts for hospitals), in subsection (3)(d), after "case, the" there is inserted "Strategic Health Authority,".

26   In section 92 (further transfers of trust property) –

    (a)   in subsection (1), after "functions of any" there is inserted "Strategic Health Authority,", and

    (b)   in subsection (1A), before paragraph (a) there is inserted –

        "(za)   a Strategic Health Authority;".

27   In section 96 (trusts: supplementary provisions), in subsection (1A)(a), after "or a" there is inserted "Strategic Health Authority,".

28   In section 96A (power of health authorities, etc to raise money) –

    (a)   in subsection (1), before "Health Authority,", in both places, there is inserted "Strategic Health Authority,",

    (b)   in subsection (3), after "benefit of the" there is inserted "Strategic Health Authority,",

    (c)   in subsection (4), before "Health Authority," there is inserted "Strategic Health Authority,",

    (d)   in subsection (5)(b), before "Health Authority" there is inserted "Strategic Health Authority,", and

    (e)   in each of subsections (7), (8) and (9), before "Health Authority,", in each place where it occurs, there is inserted "Strategic Health Authority,".

29   In section 98 (accounts and audit) –

National Health Service Reform and Health Care Professions Act 2002 (c. 17)
Schedule 1 – English Health Authorities: change of name
Part 1 – Amendments of 1977 Act

53

(a) in subsection (1), before paragraph (a) there is inserted —

"(za)   every Strategic Health Authority;", and

(b) in subsection (2AA), for "Health Authority" there is substituted "Strategic Health Authority".

30   In section 99 (regulation of financial arrangements), in subsection (1), before paragraph (a) there is inserted —

"(za)   Strategic Health Authorities,".

31   In section 125 (protection of members and officers of authorities), before paragraph (a) there is inserted —

"(za)   a Strategic Health Authority;".

32   In section 126 (orders and regulations, and directions), in subsection (3A), after "or by a" there is inserted "Strategic Health Authority or".

33   In section 128 (interpretation and construction), in subsection (1A), before "Health Authority,", in both places, there is inserted "Strategic Health Authority,".

34   (1) Schedule 5 (which relates to the constitution of Health Authorities and Special Health Authorities) is amended as provided in this paragraph.

(2) In Part 1 (membership of Health Authorities) —

(a) for "Health Authority", in each place where it occurs, there is substituted "Strategic Health Authority",

(b) in paragraph 4, for "Health Authorities" there is substituted "Strategic Health Authorities",

(c) after paragraph 4 there is inserted —

"4A   Paragraphs 1 to 4 above apply in relation to Health Authorities as they apply in relation to Strategic Health Authorities.", and

(d) in the heading, for "Membership of Health Authorities" there is substituted "Membership of Strategic Health Authorities and Health Authorities".

(3) In Part 3 (supplementary provisions) —

(a) in paragraph 8, after "Each" there is inserted "Strategic Health Authority, each", and

(b) in paragraph 9, in sub-paragraph (7)(a), before "Health Authority" there is inserted "Strategic Health Authority or".

35   (1) Schedule 5A (which relates to Primary Care Trusts) is amended as provided in this paragraph.

(2) In Part 2 (Constitution and Membership), in paragraph 10, after "in relation to" there is inserted "Strategic Health Authorities,".

(3) In Part 3 (Powers and duties), in paragraph 20, for "Health Authority" there is substituted "Strategic Health Authority".

(4) In Part 4 (Transfer of property), in paragraph 21, for "Health Authority" (in each place where it occurs) there is substituted "Strategic Health Authority".

(5) In Part 5 (Transfer of staff), in paragraph 23(2), for paragraph (a) there is substituted —

"(a)   a Strategic Health Authority,".

54

National Health Service Reform and Health Care Professions Act 2002 (c. 17)
Schedule 1 – English Health Authorities: change of name
Part 2 – Amendments of other Acts

PART 2

AMENDMENTS OF OTHER ACTS

The Reserve and Auxiliary Forces (Protection of Civil Interests) Act 1951 (c. 65)

36   In Part 1 of Schedule 2 to the Reserve and Auxiliary Forces (Protection of Civil Interests) Act 1951 (which makes provision about payments to make up civil remuneration), in paragraph 15 –

    (a)   in the entry in the first column, before "a Health Authority" there is inserted "a Strategic Health Authority,", and

    (b)   in the entry in the second column, before "Health Authority" there is inserted "Strategic Health Authority,".

The Hospital Complaints Procedure Act 1985 (c. 42)

37   In section 1 of the Hospital Complaints Procedure Act 1985 (hospital complaints procedure), in subsection (1) –

    (a)   for "Health Authority and" there is substituted "Strategic Health Authority and Health Authority, to each", and

    (b)   after "which that" there is inserted "Strategic Health Authority,".

The Disabled Persons (Services, Consultation and Representation) Act 1986 (c. 33)

38   (1)   The Disabled Persons (Services, Consultation and Representation) Act 1986 is amended as provided in this paragraph.

    (2)   In section 7 (persons discharged from hospital), in subsection (9), in paragraph (a) of the definition of "the managers", after "means the" there is inserted "Strategic Health Authority,".

    (3)   In section 16 (interpretation), after the definition of "statutory services" there is inserted –

> " "Strategic Health Authority" means a Strategic Health Authority established under section 8 of the 1977 Act;".

The National Health Service and Community Care Act 1990 (c. 19)

39   The National Health Service and Community Care Act 1990 is amended as follows.

40   In section 4 (NHS contracts), in subsection (2), before paragraph (a) there is inserted –

> "(za)   a Strategic Health Authority;".

41   In section 4A (provision of certain services by persons on ophthalmic or pharmaceutical lists), in subsection (1), after "under which" there is inserted "a Strategic Health Authority,".

42   In section 8 (transfer of property, rights and liabilities to NHS trusts), before "Health Authority", in each place where it occurs, there is inserted "Strategic Health Authority,".

43   In section 21 (schemes for meeting losses and liabilities of certain health service bodies) –

National Health Service Reform and Health Care Professions Act 2002 (c. 17)
Schedule 1 – English Health Authorities: change of name
Part 2 – Amendments of other Acts

55

    (a)   in subsection (2), before paragraph (a) there is inserted –

        "(za)   Strategic Health Authorities;", and

    (b)   in each of subsections (3), (4) and (5), before "Health Authority" there is inserted "Strategic Health Authority,".

44   In section 49 (transfer of staff from health service to local authorities), in subsection (4)(b), after "means a" there is inserted "Strategic Health Authority,".

45   In section 60 (removal of Crown immunities), in subsection (7)(a), at the beginning there is inserted "a Strategic Health Authority or".

46   In Schedule 2 (which makes provision about NHS trusts) –

    (a)   in each of paragraphs 4(1), 4(2), 5(3), 13, 30(2) and 31, before "Health Authority" there is inserted "Strategic Health Authority,", and

    (b)   in paragraph 30(1), after paragraph (a) there is inserted –

        "(aa)   a Strategic Health Authority, or".

The Health Service Commissioners Act 1993 (c. 46)

47   In section 2 of the Health Service Commissioners Act 1993 (bodies subject to investigation), in subsection (1), for paragraph (a) there is substituted –

        "(a)   Strategic Health Authorities,".

The 1999 Act

48   The 1999 Act is amended as follows.

49   In section 20 (functions of the Commission for Health Improvement) –

    (a)   in subsection (1)(c), before "Health Authorities" there is inserted "Strategic Health Authorities,", and

    (b)   in subsection (7), in the definition of "NHS body", after "means a" there is inserted "Strategic Health Authority,".

50   In section 21 (arrangements with the Audit Commission), in subsection (1)(b)(iii), after "relate to" there is inserted "Strategic Health Authorities,".

51   In section 26 (co-operation between NHS bodies), after "duty of" there is inserted "Strategic Health Authorities,".

52   In section 28 (plans for improving health etc) –

    (a)   in subsection (6) –

        (i)   in paragraphs (b) and (g), before "Health Authorities" there is inserted "Strategic Health Authorities,", and

        (ii)   in paragraph (h), after "provision by" there is inserted "Strategic Health Authorities,", and

    (b)   in subsection (9), after "duty of" there is inserted "Strategic Health Authorities,".

53   In section 31 (arrangements between NHS bodies and local authorities), in subsection (8), in the definition of "NHS body", after "means a" there is inserted "Strategic Health Authority,".

54   In section 61 (English and Scottish border provisions), in subsection (2), for "Health Authority" there is substituted "Strategic Health Authority".

56   *National Health Service Reform and Health Care Professions Act 2002 (c. 17)*
Schedule 1 – English Health Authorities: change of name
Part 2 – Amendments of other Acts

The Health and Social Care Act 2001 (c. 15)

55   (1) The Health and Social Care Act 2001 is amended as provided in this
         paragraph.

     (2) In section 7 (functions of overview and scrutiny committees), in subsection
         (4), after "means a" there is inserted "Strategic Health Authority,".

     (3) In section 46 (directed partnership arrangements), in subsection (5), in the
         definition of "NHS body", after "means a" there is inserted "Strategic Health
         Authority,".

SCHEDULE 2   Section 2(5)

REALLOCATION OF FUNCTIONS OF HEALTH AUTHORITIES TO PRIMARY CARE TRUSTS

PART 1

AMENDMENTS OF 1977 ACT

1   The 1977 Act is amended as follows.

2   (1) Section 15 (duty of Health Authority in relation to family health services) is
         amended as provided in this paragraph.

     (2) In subsection (1), after "duty" there is inserted "of each Primary Care Trust
         and".

     (3) In subsection (1B) –
         (a) before "Health Authority", in each place where it occurs, there is
              inserted "Primary Care Trust or",
         (b) for "that Authority's medical list" there is substituted "the medical
              list of that Trust or Authority", and
         (c) for "that Authority" there is substituted "that Trust or Authority".

     (4) In subsection (1BA) –
         (a) after "relevant" there is inserted "Primary Care Trust or", and
         (b) for "the Authority" there is substituted "the Trust or Authority".

     (5) Sub-paragraphs (3) and (4), and this sub-paragraph, shall cease to have
         effect on the coming into force of paragraph 8 of Schedule 4 to the 1999 Act
         (which repeals subsections (1B) to (1D) of section 15 of the 1977 Act).

3   (1) Section 29 (arrangements and regulations for general medical services) is
         amended as provided in this paragraph.

     (2) In subsection (1), after "duty" there is inserted "of every Primary Care Trust
         and".

     (3) In subsection (2) –
         (a) for paragraph (a) there is substituted –
                   "(a) for the preparation and publication by each Primary
                        Care Trust and by each Health Authority of a list of
                        medical practitioners who undertake to provide
                        general medical services for persons in the area of the
                        Primary Care Trust or Health Authority;", and

National Health Service Reform and Health Care Professions Act 2002 (c. 17)
Schedule 2 – Reallocation of functions of Health Authorities to Primary Care Trusts
Part 1 – Amendments of 1977 Act

57

      (b)   in paragraph (f), after "of a" there is inserted "Primary Care Trust or".

4   (1)   Section 29A (medical lists) is amended as provided in this paragraph.

    (2)   For subsection (1) there is substituted –

> "(1)   A Primary Care Trust or Health Authority may not, under section 29, arrange with a medical practitioner for him to provide general medical services for persons in the area of the Trust or Authority unless his name is included in the medical list of the Trust or Authority."

    (3)   In subsection (2) –

      (a)   for "a Health Authority's medical list" there is substituted "the medical list of a Primary Care Trust or Health Authority", and

      (b)   in paragraph (b), after "of the" there is inserted "Trust or".

    (4)   In subsection (3)(b), for "all Health Authorities' medical lists" there is substituted "the medical lists of all Primary Care Trusts and Health Authorities".

    (5)   In subsection (4A), after "to a" there is inserted "Primary Care Trust or".

    (6)   In subsection (6) –

      (a)   after "to a" there is inserted "Primary Care Trust or", and

      (b)   after "by the" there is inserted "Trust or".

5   (1)   Section 29B (vacancies for medical practitioners) is amended as provided in this paragraph.

    (2)   In each of subsections (2) and (2A), before "Health Authority", in each place where it occurs, there is inserted "Primary Care Trust or".

    (3)   In subsection (3) –

      (a)   in paragraph (aa), after "which a" there is inserted "Primary Care Trust or",

      (b)   the "or" at the end of paragraph (b) is omitted, and

      (c)   for paragraph (c) there is substituted –

> "(c)   vacancies relating to the area of one Primary Care Trust which also relate to the area of another Primary Care Trust, or of a Health Authority, or of a Health Board, or
>
> (d)   vacancies relating to the area of one Health Authority which also relate to the area of another Health Authority or of a Primary Care Trust,".

    (4)   In subsection (3A) –

      (a)   after "that a" there is inserted "Primary Care Trust or", and

      (b)   for "Health Authority's decision" there is substituted "decision of the Primary Care Trust or of the Health Authority".

    (5)   In subsection (5), for the definition of "locality" there is substituted –

> " "locality", in relation to a Primary Care Trust or to a Health Authority, means the area of the Trust or of the Authority, or a particular part of their area;".

6   In section 31 (requirement of suitable experience), in subsection (1), after "by a" there is inserted "Primary Care Trust or".

58   *National Health Service Reform and Health Care Professions Act 2002 (c. 17)*
Schedule 2 — Reallocation of functions of Health Authorities to Primary Care Trusts
Part 1 — Amendments of 1977 Act

7   In section 32 (regulations as to section 31), in subsection (1), in the definition of "applicant", after "by a" there is inserted "Primary Care Trust or".

8   In section 33 (distribution of general medical services) —

     (a)   in subsection (1A)(a), for "Health Authorities for areas in England" there is substituted "Primary Care Trusts", and

     (b)   in subsection (1A)(b), "for areas in Wales" is omitted.

9   In section 35 (arrangements for general dental services), in subsection (1), after "duty" there is inserted "of every Primary Care Trust and".

10   (1)   Section 36 (regulations as to section 35) is amended as provided in this paragraph.

    (2)   In subsection (1), for paragraph (a) there is substituted —

       "(a)   for the preparation and publication by each Primary Care Trust and by each Health Authority of a list of dental practitioners and dental corporations who undertake to provide general dental services for persons in the area of the Primary Care Trust or Health Authority;".

    (3)   In subsection (1A), before "Health Authority", in both places, there is inserted "Primary Care Trust or".

    (4)   In subsection (2) —

     (a)   before "Health Authority", in both places, there is inserted "Primary Care Trust or", and

     (b)   for "Health Authority's area" there is substituted "area of the Primary Care Trust or Health Authority".

    (5)   In subsection (4), after "which a" there is inserted "Primary Care Trust or".

    (6)   In subsection (6) —

     (a)   after "that a" there is inserted "Primary Care Trust or", and

     (b)   for "Health Authority's decision" there is substituted "decision of the Primary Care Trust or of the Health Authority".

    (7)   In each of subsections (7) and (8), before "Health Authority", in each place where it occurs, there is inserted "Primary Care Trust or".

11   In section 38 (arrangements for general ophthalmic services), in subsection (1), after "duty" there is inserted "of every Primary Care Trust and".

12   (1)   Section 39 (regulations as to section 38) is amended as provided in this paragraph.

    (2)   In subsection (1), for paragraph (a) there is substituted —

       "(a)   for the preparation and publication by each Primary Care Trust and by each Health Authority of a list of medical practitioners and a list of ophthalmic opticians who undertake to provide general ophthalmic services for persons in the area of the Primary Care Trust or Health Authority;".

    (3)   In subsection (2), before "Health Authority", in each place where it occurs, there is inserted "Primary Care Trust or".

    (4)   In subsection (3) —

     (a)   after "that a" there is inserted "Primary Care Trust or", and

     (b)   for "Health Authority's decision" there is substituted "decision of the Primary Care Trust or of the Health Authority".

National Health Service Reform and Health Care Professions Act 2002 (c. 17)
Schedule 2 – Reallocation of functions of Health Authorities to Primary Care Trusts
Part 1 – Amendments of 1977 Act

59

13 (1) Section 41 (arrangements for pharmaceutical services) is amended as provided in this paragraph.

(2) In subsection (1), after "duty" there is inserted "of every Primary Care Trust and".

(3) In each of subsections (5) and (6), before "Health Authority", in each place where it occurs, there is inserted "Primary Care Trust or".

14 In section 41A (additional pharmaceutical services), before "Health Authority", in each place where it occurs, there is inserted "Primary Care Trust or".

15 In section 41B (terms and conditions relating to additional pharmaceutical services), before "Health Authority", in each place where it occurs, there is inserted "Primary Care Trust or".

16 (1) Section 42 (regulations as to pharmaceutical services) is amended as provided in this paragraph.

(2) In subsection (1), before "Health Authority" there is inserted "Primary Care Trust or".

(3) In subsection (2) –

(a) before "Health Authority", in each place where it occurs, there is inserted "Primary Care Trust or", and

(b) in paragraph (a), for "Health Authority's area" there is substituted "area of the Primary Care Trust or Health Authority".

(4) In subsection (3) –

(a) before "Health Authority", in each place where it occurs, there is inserted "Primary Care Trust or", and

(b) in paragraph (ba), for "Health Authority's area" there is substituted "area of the Primary Care Trust or Health Authority".

(5) In subsection (3B)(b), before "Health Authority" there is inserted "Primary Care Trust or".

(6) In subsection (4A) –

(a) before "Health Authority" there is inserted "Primary Care Trust or", and

(b) for "Health Authority's decision" there is substituted "decision of the Primary Care Trust or of the Health Authority".

17 (1) Section 43 (persons authorised to provide pharmaceutical services) is amended as provided in this paragraph.

(2) In subsection (1), before "Health Authority" there is inserted "Primary Care Trust or".

(3) For subsection (2A) there is substituted –

"(2A) Regulations shall provide for the preparation and publication by each Primary Care Trust and by each Health Authority of one or more lists of medical practitioners who undertake to provide drugs, medicines or listed appliances under arrangements with the Primary Care Trust or with the Health Authority."

(4) In subsection (2BA), before "Health Authority", in each place where it occurs, there is inserted "Primary Care Trust or".

(5) In subsection (2BB) –

60

National Health Service Reform and Health Care Professions Act 2002 (c. 17)
Schedule 2 — Reallocation of functions of Health Authorities to Primary Care Trusts
Part 1 — Amendments of 1977 Act

     (a) before "Health Authority" there is inserted "Primary Care Trust or", and

     (b) for "Health Authority's decision" there is substituted "decision of the Primary Care Trust or of the Health Authority".

18 (1) Section 43ZA (conditional inclusion in medical, dental, ophthalmic and pharmaceutical lists) is amended as provided in this paragraph.

    (2) In subsection (1)—

     (a) in paragraph (a), for "Health Authority" there is substituted "Primary Care Trust or Health Authority in whose list he is included", and

     (b) before "Health Authority", in each other place where it occurs, there is inserted "Primary Care Trust or".

    (3) In subsection (4)—

     (a) before "Health Authority", in each place where it occurs, there is inserted "Primary Care Trust or", and

     (b) in paragraph (b)(iii), for "Health Authority's decision" there is substituted "decision of the Primary Care Trust or of the Health Authority".

    (4) In subsection (5), for "Health Authority's decision", in both places, there is substituted "decision of the Primary Care Trust or of the Health Authority".

    (5) In subsection (7), before "Health Authority" there is inserted "Primary Care Trust or".

19 In section 43C (indemnity cover for Part 2 practitioners), before "Health Authority", in each place where it occurs, there is inserted "Primary Care Trust or".

20 (1) Section 43D (supplementary lists) is amended as provided in this paragraph.

    (2) In subsection (1)—

     (a) after "publication by" there is inserted "each Primary Care Trust and", and

     (b) after "by the" there is inserted "Primary Care Trust or".

    (3) In subsection (3)—

     (a) before "Health Authority", in each place where it occurs, there is inserted "Primary Care Trust or", and

     (b) in paragraph (j), before "Health Authorities" there is inserted "Primary Care Trusts and".

    (4) In subsection (4), before "Health Authority", in each place where it occurs, there is inserted "Primary Care Trust or".

    (5) In subsection (7)—

     (a) before "Health Authority", in both places, there is inserted "Primary Care Trust or", and

     (b) for "Health Authority's decision" there is substituted "decision of the Primary Care Trust or of the Health Authority".

    (6) In subsection (8)—

     (a) before "Health Authority" there is inserted "Primary Care Trust or", and

     (b) for "Health Authority's decision" there is substituted "decision of the Primary Care Trust or of the Health Authority".

National Health Service Reform and Health Care Professions Act 2002 (c. 17)
Schedule 2 – Reallocation of functions of Health Authorities to Primary Care Trusts
Part 1 – Amendments of 1977 Act

61

    (7) In subsection (9), for "Health Authority's decision" there is substituted "decision of the Primary Care Trust or of the Health Authority".

    (8) In subsection (10), after "by a" there is inserted "Primary Care Trust or".

    (9) In subsection (11)—

        (a) in paragraph (a), after "prepared" there is inserted "by the same Primary Care Trust or", and

        (b) in paragraph (b)—

            (i) for "Health Authorities in England" there is substituted "Primary Care Trusts", and

            (ii) for "Health Authorities in Wales" there is substituted "Health Authorities".

21   In each of the following—

        (a) section 49F (disqualification of practitioners),

        (b) section 49G (contingent removal), and

        (c) section 49I (suspension),

      before "Health Authority", in each place where it occurs, there is inserted "Primary Care Trust or".

22   In section 49J (suspension pending appeal)—

        (a) before "Health Authority", in each place where it occurs, there is inserted "Primary Care Trust or", and

        (b) in subsection (6), for "Health Authority's decision" there is substituted "decision of the Primary Care Trust or of the Health Authority".

23   In section 49L (review of decisions)—

        (a) in subsections (1) and (3), before "Health Authority" there is inserted "Primary Care Trust or", and

        (b) in subsection (2), for "Health Authority's decision" there is substituted "decision of the Primary Care Trust or of the Health Authority".

24   In section 49M (appeals)—

        (a) before "Health Authority", in each place where it occurs, there is inserted "Primary Care Trust or",

        (b) in subsection (3), for "Health Authority's decision" there is substituted "decision of the Primary Care Trust or of the Health Authority", and

        (c) in subsection (7), after "payments by" there is inserted "Primary Care Trusts and".

25 (1) Section 49N (national disqualification) is amended as provided in this paragraph.

    (2) In subsection (1)—

        (a) before "all Health Authorities", in each place where it occurs, there is inserted "all Primary Care Trusts and", and

        (b) in paragraph (c), before "any Health Authority" there is inserted "any Primary Care Trust or".

    (3) In subsection (3), for "a Health Authority's refusal" there is substituted "the refusal by a Primary Care Trust or Health Authority".

62   *National Health Service Reform and Health Care Professions Act 2002 (c. 17)*
Schedule 2 – Reallocation of functions of Health Authorities to Primary Care Trusts
Part 1 – Amendments of 1977 Act

(4) In subsection (4), before "Health Authority" there is inserted "Primary Care Trust or".

(5) In subsection (6) –

    (a) in paragraph (a), after "no" there is inserted "Primary Care Trust or", and

    (b) in paragraph (b), after "a list," there is inserted "each Primary Care Trust and".

26   In section 49O (notification of decisions), after "require a" there is inserted "Primary Care Trust or".

27   In section 49P (withdrawal from lists), after "whom a", in both places, there is inserted "Primary Care Trust or".

28 (1) Section 49Q (regulations) is amended as provided in this paragraph.

    (2) In subsection (1), after "by a" there is inserted "Primary Care Trust or".

    (3) In subsection (2) –

        (a) in paragraph (b), after "before a" there is inserted "Primary Care Trust or", and

        (b) in paragraph (c), for "Health Authority's decision" there is substituted "decision of the Primary Care Trust or of the Health Authority".

    (4) In subsection (3), after "which the" there is inserted "Primary Care Trust or".

29   In section 54, after "Committee", in each place where it occurs, there is inserted ", Primary Care Trust".

30   In section 56 (inadequate Part 2 services) –

    (a) before "Health Authority", where it first occurs, there is inserted "Primary Care Trust or", and

    (b) in paragraph (i), after "authorise the" there is inserted "Primary Care Trust or".

31   In section 83 (sums otherwise payable to those providing services), before "Health Authority", in the second place where it occurs, there is inserted "Primary Care Trust or".

32   In section 83A (remission and repayment of charges and travelling expenses), in subsection (1) –

    (a) after paragraph (b) there is inserted –

        "(ba) for the reimbursement by a Primary Care Trust to an NHS trust and, in such cases as may be prescribed, to a Health Authority or another Primary Care Trust, of payments made by virtue of exercising the functions conferred under paragraph (b) above; and", and

    (b) in paragraph (c), for "of payments" to the end there is substituted "of such payments."

33   In section 92 (transfers of property held on trust), in subsection (1), after "Strategic Health Authority," (inserted by paragraph 26 of Schedule 1 to this Act) there is inserted "Primary Care Trust,".

34   In section 96A (powers of health authorities, etc, to raise money by appeals, etc), in subsection (5)(b), after "Strategic Health Authority," (inserted by

National Health Service Reform and Health Care Professions Act 2002 (c. 17)
Schedule 2 — Reallocation of functions of Health Authorities to Primary Care Trusts
Part 1 — Amendments of 1977 Act

63

paragraph 28(d) of Schedule 1 to this Act) there is inserted "Primary Care Trust or".

35   In section 103 (special arrangement as to payment of remuneration), in subsection (3)(a) —

(a)   "or a Primary Care Trust" is omitted, and

(b)   for "Health Authority" there is substituted "Primary Care Trust, Health Authority or Local Health Board".

36   (1)   Section 124 (special notices of births and deaths) is amended as provided in this paragraph.

(2)   Before "Health Authority", in each place where it occurs, there is inserted "Primary Care Trust or".

(3)   In subsection (2), for "Health Authority's area" there is substituted "area of the Primary Care Trust or Health Authority".

(4)   In subsection (5), for "Health Authority's offices" there is substituted "offices of the Primary Care Trust or of the Health Authority".

37   In Schedule 5A (which relates to Primary Care Trusts), after paragraph 10 there is inserted —

"10A   Where the registration of a dentist in the dentist's register is suspended —

(a)   by an order under section 32 of the Dentists Act 1984 (interim suspension); or

(b)   by a direction or order of the Health Committee under that Act (health cases),

the suspension shall not terminate any contract of employment made between him and a Primary Care Trust, but a person whose registration is so suspended shall not perform any duties under a contract made between him and a Primary Care Trust which involves the practice of dentistry within the meaning of that Act."

PART 2

AMENDMENTS OF OTHER ACTS

The National Assistance Act 1948 (c. 29)

38   In section 26 of the National Assistance Act 1948 (provision of accommodation in premises maintained by voluntary organisations), in subsection (1C), after "consent of such" there is inserted "Primary Care Trust or".

The Reserve and Auxiliary Forces (Protection of Civil Interests) Act 1951 (c. 65)

39   In Part 1 of Schedule 2 to the Reserve and Auxiliary Forces (Protection of Civil Interests) Act 1951 (which makes provision about payments to make up civil remuneration), in paragraph 16, in the entry in the second column, before "Health Authority" there is inserted "Primary Care Trust,".

The Health Services and Public Health Act 1968 (c. 46)

40   (1)   The Health Services and Public Health Act 1968 is amended as provided in this paragraph.

64   *National Health Service Reform and Health Care Professions Act 2002 (c. 17)*
            Schedule 2 — Reallocation of functions of Health Authorities to Primary Care Trusts
                                              Part 2 — Amendments of other Acts

(2) In section 63 (provision of instruction for certain persons), in subsection (2)(b), before "Health Authority" there is inserted "Primary Care Trust or".

(3) In section 64 (financial assistance to certain voluntary organisations), in subsection (3)(b), before "Health Authority" there is inserted "Primary Care Trust or".

The Health and Safety at Work etc Act 1974 (c. 37)

41   In section 60 of the Health and Safety at Work etc Act 1974 (which makes supplementary provision in relation to the employment medical advisory service), in subsection (1), after "that each" there is inserted "Primary Care Trust and".

The Mental Health Act 1983 (c. 20)

42   The Mental Health Act 1983 is amended as follows.

43   In section 25A (applications for supervision), before "Health Authority", in each place where it occurs, there is inserted "Primary Care Trust or".

44   In section 25C (supervision applications: supplementary), in subsection (6), after "consent of the" there is inserted "Primary Care Trust or".

45   In section 25F (reclassification of patient subject to after-care under supervision), in subsection (1), after "effect to the" there is inserted "Primary Care Trust or".

46   In section 39 (information as to hospitals), in subsection (1), before "Health Authority", in each place where it occurs, there is inserted "Primary Care Trust or".

47   In section 117 (after-care), in each of subsections (2), (2A) and (3), before "Health Authority", in each place where it occurs, there is inserted "Primary Care Trust or".

48   In section 140 (notification of hospitals having arrangements for reception of urgent cases) —
      (a) after "duty of" there is inserted "every Primary Care Trust and of",
      (b) for "Health Authority's area" there is substituted "area of the Primary Care Trust or Health Authority", and
      (c) after "available to the" there is inserted "Primary Care Trust or".

49   In section 145 (interpretation), in paragraph (a) of the definition of "the managers", before "Health Authority" there is inserted "Primary Care Trust,".

The Public Health (Control of Disease) Act 1984 (c. 22)

50   (1) The Public Health (Control of Disease) Act 1984 is amended as provided in this paragraph.

(2) In section 11 (cases of notifiable disease and food poisoning to be reported), before "Health Authority", in each place where it occurs, there is inserted "Primary Care Trust or".

(3) In section 12 (fees for certificates under section 11), in subsection (1), after "that a" there is inserted "Primary Care Trust or".

National Health Service Reform and Health Care Professions Act 2002 (c. 17)
Schedule 2 – Reallocation of functions of Health Authorities to Primary Care Trusts
Part 2 – Amendments of other Acts

65

(4) In section 39 (keeper of common lodging-house to notify case of infectious disease), in subsection (3), after "to the" there is inserted "Primary Care Trust or".

The Disabled Persons (Services, Consultation and Representation) Act 1986 (c. 33)

51 In section 7 of the Disabled Persons (Services, Consultation and Representation) Act 1986 (persons discharged from hospital), in subsection (9), for paragraph (a) of the definition of "health authority" there is substituted—

"(a) in relation to England, means a Primary Care Trust,

(aa) in relation to Wales, means a Health Authority, and".

The Children Act 1989 (c. 41)

52 In Schedule 2 to the Children Act 1989 (local authority support for children and families), in paragraph 1A(3)(a), for "and" there is substituted "or".

The National Health Service and Community Care Act 1990 (c. 19)

53 The National Health Service and Community Care Act 1990 is amended as follows.

54 In section 4A (provision of certain services by persons on ophthalmic or pharmaceutical lists), in subsection (1), after "a Strategic Health Authority," (inserted by paragraph 41 of Schedule 1 to this Act) there is inserted "a Primary Care Trust,".

55 (1) In section 18 (indicative amounts for doctors' practices)—

(a) in subsection (1)—

(i) after "financial year," there is inserted "every Primary Care Trust and", and

(ii) before "Health Authority", in the second and third places it occurs, there is inserted "Primary Care Trust or",

(b) before "Health Authority", in each other place where it occurs except in subsection (7), there is inserted "Primary Care Trust or", and

(c) in subsection (7), for "Health Authority" there is substituted "Primary Care Trust".

(2) This paragraph shall cease to have effect on the coming into force of paragraph 80 of Schedule 4 to the 1999 Act (which repeals section 18 of the National Health Service and Community Care Act 1990).

56 In section 47 (assessment of needs for community care services), in subsection (3)—

(a) before "Health Authority", where it first occurs, there is inserted "Primary Care Trust or", and

(b) before "Health Authority", in each other place where it occurs, there is inserted "Primary Care Trust,".

57 In section 49 (transfer of staff from health service to local authorities), in subsection (4)(b), after "Strategic Health Authority," (inserted by paragraph 44 of Schedule 1 to this Act) there is inserted "Primary Care Trust,".

66

National Health Service Reform and Health Care Professions Act 2002 (c. 17)
Schedule 2 – Reallocation of functions of Health Authorities to Primary Care Trusts
Part 2 – Amendments of other Acts

58   In Schedule 2 (which makes provision about NHS trusts), in paragraph 31, after "Strategic Health Authority" (inserted by paragraph 46 of Schedule 1 to this Act) there is inserted "Primary Care Trust,".

The Access to Health Records Act 1990 (c. 23)

59   (1) The Access to Health Records Act 1990 is amended as provided in this paragraph.

      (2) In section 1 (definitions of certain terms), in subsection (2)(a)(ii), before "Health Authority" there is inserted "Primary Care Trust,".

      (3) In section 7 (duty of health service bodies etc to take advice), before "Health Authority", in each place where it occurs, there is inserted "Primary Care Trust,".

The Trade Union and Labour Relations (Consolidation) Act 1992 (c. 52)

60   In section 279 of the Trade Union and Labour Relations (Consolidation) Act 1992 (health service practitioners), in paragraph (a), before "Health Authority" there is inserted "Primary Care Trust or".

The Health Service Commissioners Act 1993 (c. 46)

61   (1) The Health Service Commissioners Act 1993 is amended as provided in this paragraph.

      (2) In section 2 (bodies subject to investigation) –
          (a) in subsection (1), in paragraph (da), "established for areas in England" is omitted, and
          (b) in subsection (2), in paragraph (a), "whose areas are in Wales" is omitted.

      (3) In section 6 (which provides for certain action by Health Authorities, etc not to be investigated), in each of subsections (3) and (5), after "taken by a" there is inserted "Primary Care Trust or".

The Health Authorities Act 1995 (c. 17)

62   In Schedule 2 to the Health Authorities Act 1995 (transitional provisions and savings), in paragraph 2, before "Health Authority", in each place where it occurs, there is inserted "Primary Care Trust,".

The Employment Rights Act 1996 (c. 18)

63   In section 43K of the Employment Rights Act 1996 (extended meaning of "worker" for Part 4A of that Act), in subsection (1)(c)(i), before "Health Authority" there is inserted "Primary Care Trust or".

The Police Act 1997 (c. 50)

64   In section 115 of the Police Act 1997 (enhanced criminal record certificates), in subsection (6E), before "Health Authority", in both places, there is inserted "Primary Care Trust or".

National Health Service Reform and Health Care Professions Act 2002 (c. 17)   67
Schedule 2 – Reallocation of functions of Health Authorities to Primary Care Trusts
Part 2 – Amendments of other Acts

The School Standards and Framework Act 1998 (c. 31)

65   In Schedule 9 to the School Standards and Framework Act 1998 (which provides for the constitution of school governing bodies), in paragraph 10 (community special schools), in sub-paragraph (5)(a), after "by the" there is inserted "Primary Care Trust or".

The Government of Wales Act 1998 (c. 38)

66   (1) The Government of Wales Act 1998 is amended as provided in this paragraph.

      (2) In Schedule 5 (bodies and offices covered by section 74), in paragraph 20, "for an area in, or consisting of, Wales" is omitted.

      (3) In Schedule 17 (audit, etc, of Welsh public bodies), in paragraph 12, "for an area in, or consisting of, Wales" is omitted.

The 1999 Act

67   The 1999 Act is amended as follows.

68   In section 10(1) (which substitutes new sections 43A and 43B in the 1977 Act), in the new section 43A (remuneration for Part 2 services), in subsection (2)(b), after "Health Authority" there is inserted ", Primary Care Trust".

69   (1) Section 28 (plans for improving health care, etc) is amended as follows.

      (2) In each of subsections (1) and (2), after "Health Authority" there is inserted "and each Primary Care Trust".

      (3) In subsection (3), after "Health Authority" there is inserted "or Primary Care Trust".

      (4) For subsection (4) there is substituted —

             "(4)   Those bodies are—
                     (a)   any local authority whose area falls wholly or partly within the area of the Health Authority or Primary Care Trust, and
                     (b)   if the plan is a Health Authority's, any NHS trust which provides services at or from a hospital or other establishment or facility which falls within the area of the Health Authority."

      (5) In subsection (5), after "Health Authority" there is inserted "or Primary Care Trust".

      (6) In subsection (6)(h), after "Health Authorities" there is inserted "and Primary Care Trusts".

      (7) For subsection (7) there is substituted —

             "(7)   In exercising their respective functions —
                     (a)   Health Authorities and Primary Care Trusts must have regard to any plan prepared or reviewed by them under this section,
                     (b)   Strategic Health Authorities must have regard to any plan prepared or reviewed by a Primary Care Trust any part of whose area falls within their area, and

68   *National Health Service Reform and Health Care Professions Act 2002 (c. 17)*
Schedule 2 — Reallocation of functions of Health Authorities to Primary Care Trusts
Part 2 — Amendments of other Acts

     (c)   NHS trusts and local authorities must have regard to any plan under this section in relation to which they have participated, and Primary Care Trusts must also do so in relation to plans in which they have participated by virtue of subsection (5)."

(8) In subsection (8) —

     (a)   after "Health Authority" there is inserted "or Primary Care Trust", and

     (b)   in each of paragraphs (a) and (b), for "Authority's area" there is substituted "area of the Authority or Trust".

The Care Standards Act 2000 (c. 14)

70   In section 20 of the Care Standards Act 2000 (urgent procedure for cancellation, etc of registration of establishment or agency), in subsection (6)(b), before "Health Authority" there is inserted "Primary Care Trust or".

The Health and Social Care Act 2001 (c. 15)

71   The Health and Social Care Act 2001 is amended as follows.

72   In section 18 (out of hours medical services) —

     (a)   in subsection (2), for paragraph (b) there is substituted —

         "(b)   for approval to be given, as respects out of hours services provided for persons in the area of any Primary Care Trust or Health Authority, by —

             (i)   that Primary Care Trust or Health Authority,

             (ii)   another Primary Care Trust, or

             (iii)   another Health Authority,",

     (b)   in each of paragraphs (c) and (e), before "Health Authority" there is inserted "Primary Care Trust or", and

     (c)   in paragraph (i), after "of" there is inserted "Primary Care Trusts and of".

73 (1) Section 28 (pilot schemes for local pharmaceutical services) is amended as provided in this paragraph.

  (2) In subsection (1), before "Health Authorities" there is inserted "Primary Care Trusts and".

  (3) In subsection (2), before "Health Authority", in both places, there is inserted "Primary Care Trust or".

  (4) In subsection (6) —

     (a)   after "made by" there is inserted "Primary Care Trusts and", and

     (b)   before "Health Authority" there is inserted "Primary Care Trust or".

  (5) In subsection (7), "or a Primary Care Trust" is omitted.

74   In section 30 (designation of priority neighbourhoods or premises), before "Health Authority", in both places, there is inserted "Primary Care Trust or".

75   In section 31 (reviews of pilot schemes), in subsection (3)(a), after "the" there is inserted "Primary Care Trust or".

76   In section 32 (variation and termination of pilot schemes) —

National Health Service Reform and Health Care Professions Act 2002 (c. 17)   69
Schedule 2 – Reallocation of functions of Health Authorities to Primary Care Trusts
Part 2 – Amendments of other Acts

(a)   in subsection (1), after "authorising" there is inserted "Primary Care Trusts or", and

(b)   in each of subsections (2) and (3), before "Health Authority" there is inserted "Primary Care Trust or".

77   In section 34 (funding of preparatory work) –

(a)   in subsection (1), after "regulations for" there is inserted "Primary Care Trusts and", and

(b)   in subsection (3), before "Health Authority", in both places, there is inserted "Primary Care Trust or".

78   In section 40(1) (which inserts a new section 28J into the 1977 Act), in that new section 28J (local pharmaceutical services schemes), after "made by" there is inserted "Primary Care Trusts and".

79   In Schedule 1 (exempt information relating to health services), in paragraph 10, after "by a" there is inserted "Primary Care Trust or".

80   In Schedule 2 (pilot schemes for local pharmaceutical services) –

(a)   before "Health Authority", in each place where it occurs, there is inserted "Primary Care Trust or",

(b)   in paragraph 2(5)(d), before "Health Authorities" there is inserted "Primary Care Trusts and", and

(c)   in paragraph 5(1)(a), for "Health Authority's area" there is substituted "area of the Primary Care Trust or Health Authority".

81   (1)   Schedule 3 (which inserts a new Schedule 8A into the 1977 Act) is amended as provided in this paragraph.

(2)   In the new Schedule 8A (local pharmaceutical services schemes) –

(a)   in paragraph 1(1), before "Health Authorities" there is inserted "Primary Care Trusts and",

(b)   in paragraph 1(2) –

(i)   in paragraph (a), after "by" there is inserted "a Primary Care Trust or", and

(ii)   in paragraph (c), after "other" there is inserted "Primary Care Trust or",

(c)   in paragraph 1(7), after "a" there is inserted "Primary Care Trust or",

(d)   in paragraph 1(8), "or a Primary Care Trust" is omitted,

(e)   in paragraph 2(1), after "allowing a" there is inserted "Primary Care Trust or",

(f)   in paragraph 2(2)(b), after "a" there is inserted "Primary Care Trust or",

(g)   in paragraph 3(2), after "than" there is inserted "Primary Care Trusts and", and

(h)   in paragraph 3(3)(k), after "authorise" there is inserted "Primary Care Trusts and".

82   In Schedule 5 (minor and consequential amendments), in paragraph 9, before "Health Authority", in both places, there is inserted "Primary Care Trust or".

70 *National Health Service Reform and Health Care Professions Act 2002 (c. 17)*
Schedule 3 — Amendments relating to Personal Medical Services and Personal Dental Services
Part 1 — Amendments of the National Health Service (Primary Care) Act 1997

SCHEDULE 3   Section 4(3)

AMENDMENTS RELATING TO PERSONAL MEDICAL SERVICES AND PERSONAL DENTAL
SERVICES

PART 1

AMENDMENTS OF THE NATIONAL HEALTH SERVICE (PRIMARY CARE) ACT 1997

1   The National Health Service (Primary Care) Act 1997 is amended as follows.

2   (1) Section 1 (pilot schemes) is amended as provided in this paragraph.

         (2) In subsection (6), in each of paragraphs (a) and (b), before "Health
         Authority" there is inserted "Strategic Health Authority or a".

         (3) In subsection (8), for paragraph (a) of the definition of "authority" there is
         substituted—
                   "(a) in relation to England, a Strategic Health Authority;
                   (aa) in relation to Wales, a Health Authority; and".

3   (1) Section 8ZA (lists of persons who may perform personal medical services or
         personal dental services) is amended as provided in this paragraph.

         (2) In subsection (1), after "publication" there is inserted "by each Primary Care
         Trust and".

         (3) In subsection (3)—
                   (a)   in each of paragraphs (a), (b), (c), (e), (g) and (k), before "Health
                         Authority" there is inserted "Primary Care Trust or", and
                   (b)   in paragraph (j), after "of" there is inserted "Primary Care Trusts
                         and".

         (4) In subsection (4), in each of paragraphs (a), (b) and (d), before "Health
         Authority" there is inserted "Primary Care Trust or".

         (5) In subsection (8)—
                   (a)   before "Health Authority", in both places, there is inserted "Primary
                         Care Trust or", and
                   (b)   in paragraph (c), for "Health Authority's decision" there is
                         substituted "decision of the Primary Care Trust or of the Health
                         Authority".

         (6) In subsection (9)—
                   (a)   before "Health Authority" there is inserted "Primary Care Trust or",
                         and
                   (b)   for "Health Authority's decision" there is substituted "decision of the
                         Primary Care Trust or of the Health Authority".

         (7) In subsection (10), for "Health Authority's decision" there is substituted
         "decision of the Primary Care Trust or of the Health Authority".

4   In section 8A (delegation of Health Authority functions relating to pilot
         schemes)—
                   (a)   for subsection (1) there is substituted—

                         "(1)   A Strategic Health Authority may not, under section 17A of
                                the 1977 Act, direct a Primary Care Trust to exercise any
                                functions of the Strategic Health Authority arising under a

National Health Service Reform and Health Care Professions Act 2002 (c. 17)
Schedule 3 – Amendments relating to Personal Medical Services and Personal Dental Services
Part 1 – Amendments of the National Health Service (Primary Care) Act 1997

71

pilot scheme if the Primary Care Trust is providing any services under the pilot scheme.", and

(b)   in subsection (2), for "Health Authorities", in both places, there is substituted "Strategic Health Authorities".

5   In section 12 (leaving medical lists), in subsection (2) –

(a)   for "an authority" there is substituted "a Primary Care Trust, Health Authority or Health Board", and

(b)   for "by them or by any other authority" there is substituted "by any authority".

6   (1)   Section 13 (preferential treatment on transferring to medical lists) is amended as provided in this paragraph.

(2)   In subsection (1), for "the authority's medical list" there is substituted "the medical list of the relevant body".

(3)   After subsection (1) there is inserted –

"(1A)   For the purposes of this section –

(a)   where the authority concerned is a Health Authority or a Health Board, the relevant body is that Authority or Board;

(b)   where the authority concerned is a Strategic Health Authority, the relevant body is the Primary Care Trust designated in relation to the pilot scheme by the Secretary of State."

(4)   In subsection (6), for "authority" there is substituted "relevant body".

7   (1)   Section 21(1) (which inserts new sections 28C and 28D into the 1977 Act) is amended as provided in this paragraph.

(2)   In the new section 28C (personal medical or dental services) –

(a)   in subsection (1), before "Health Authority" there is inserted "Strategic Health Authority or a",

(b)   in subsection (3), in each of paragraphs (a) and (b), after "by the" there is inserted "Primary Care Trust or", and

(c)   in subsection (6), in each of paragraphs (a) and (b), before "Health Authority" there is inserted "Strategic Health Authority or a".

(3)   In the new section 28D (persons with whom section 28C agreements may be made), in subsection (1), before "Health Authority" there is inserted "Strategic Health Authority or a".

8   In section 22(1) (which inserts a new section 28E into the 1977 Act), in that new section 28E (which provides for regulations as to personal medical or dental services) –

(a)   in subsection (2)(a), after "than" there is inserted "Strategic Health Authorities and",

(b)   in subsection (3)(k), after "authorise" there is inserted "Strategic Health Authorities and",

(c)   in subsection (7)(a), after "circumstances)" there is inserted "Primary Care Trusts and", and

(d)   in subsection (8)(a), before "Health Authority" (in both places) there is inserted "Strategic Health Authority or".

9   In section 40 (interpretation), in subsection (2), at the end of the definition of "authority" there is inserted ", except in Schedule 1".

72

National Health Service Reform and Health Care Professions Act 2002 (c. 17)
Schedule 3 — Amendments relating to Personal Medical Services and Personal Dental Services
Part 1 — Amendments of the National Health Service (Primary Care) Act 1997

10 (1) Schedule 1 (preferential treatment on transferring to medical lists) is amended as provided in this paragraph.

(2) In paragraph 1(1), for "an authority's medical list" there is substituted "the medical list of a Primary Care Trust, a Health Authority or a Health Board (in this Schedule referred to as an "authority")".

(3) In paragraph 9—

(a) after "Schedule" there is inserted ", an "authority" means a Primary Care Trust, a Health Authority or a Health Board, and", and

(b) in paragraph (a), for "a Health Authority's medical list" there is substituted "the medical list of a Primary Care Trust or of a Health Authority".

PART 2

AMENDMENTS OF OTHER ACTS

The 1977 Act

11   In section 15 of the 1977 Act (duty of Health Authority in relation to family health services), in subsection (1ZA), after "duty of" there is inserted "each Strategic Health Authority and".

The National Health Service (Scotland) Act 1978 (c. 29)

12   In the National Health Service (Scotland) Act 1978, in section 17C (personal medical or dental services)—

(a) in subsection (5), in each of paragraphs (a) and (b), before "Health Authority" there is inserted "Strategic Health Authority or by a", and

(b) in subsection (6), for the definition of "Health Authority" there is substituted—

" "Strategic Health Authority" and "Health Authority" have the same meaning as in the National Health Service Act 1977;".

The Trade Union and Labour Relations (Consolidation) Act 1992 (c. 52)

13   In section 279 of the Trade Union and Labour Relations (Consolidation) Act 1992 (health service practitioners), in paragraph (a), after "by a" there is inserted "Strategic Health Authority,".

The 1999 Act

14   In section 6(2) of the 1999 Act (which inserts a new section 28EE into the 1977 Act), in that new section 28EE—

(a) subsection (1) is omitted, and

(b) in subsection (2), for "Health Authorities", in both places, there is substituted "Strategic Health Authorities".

The Health and Social Care Act 2001 (c. 15)

15   The Health and Social Care Act 2001 is amended as follows.

16 (1) Section 26(1) (which inserts a new section 28DA into the 1977 Act) is amended as provided in this paragraph.

National Health Service Reform and Health Care Professions Act 2002 (c. 17)
Schedule 3 – Amendments relating to Personal Medical Services and Personal Dental Services
Part 2 – Amendments of other Acts

73

(2) In the new section 28DA (lists of persons who may perform personal medical services or personal dental services) –

    (a) in subsection (1), after "publication" there is inserted "by each Primary Care Trust and",

    (b) in subsection (3) –

        (i) in each of paragraphs (a), (b), (c), (e), (g) and (k), before "Health Authority" there is inserted "Primary Care Trust or", and

        (ii) in paragraph (j), after "of" there is inserted "Primary Care Trusts and",

    (c) in subsection (4), in each of paragraphs (a), (b) and (d), before "Health Authority" there is inserted "Primary Care Trust or",

    (d) in subsection (8) –

        (i) before "Health Authority", in both places, there is inserted "Primary Care Trust or", and

        (ii) in paragraph (c), for "Health Authority's decision" there is substituted "decision of the Primary Care Trust or of the Health Authority",

    (e) in subsection (9) –

        (i) before "Health Authority" there is inserted "Primary Care Trust or", and

        (ii) for "Health Authority's decision" there is substituted "decision of the Primary Care Trust or of the Health Authority", and

    (f) in subsection (10), for "Health Authority's decision" there is substituted "decision of the Primary Care Trust or of the Health Authority".

17   In Schedule 1 (exempt information relating to health services), in paragraph 11, after "request to a" there is inserted "Strategic Health Authority or".

SCHEDULE 4

Section 6(2)

LOCAL HEALTH BOARDS

After Schedule 5A to the 1977 Act there is inserted –

"SCHEDULE 5B

LOCAL HEALTH BOARDS

PART 1

LHB ORDERS

1   (1) An LHB order shall specify –

    (a) the name of the Board; and

    (b) the operational date of the Board.

(2) The operational date of a Local Health Board is the date on which functions exercisable by it may first be undertaken fully by the Board.

2   (1) An LHB order may provide for the establishment of a Local Health Board with effect from a date earlier than the operational date.

(2) During the period beginning with that earlier date and ending with the day immediately preceding the operational date (referred to in this Schedule as the preparatory period), the exercise of any functions by the Board shall be limited to such exercise as may be specified in the LHB order for the purpose of enabling it to begin to operate satisfactorily with effect from the operational date.

(3) Sub-paragraphs (4) and (5) below apply for so long as there is a Health Authority for any part of the area of Wales specified in a particular LHB order.

(4) That LHB order may require such a Health Authority to meet the costs of the Board performing its functions during the preparatory period by doing either or both of the following—

(a) discharging such liabilities of the Board as may be incurred during the preparatory period and are of a description specified in the order;

(b) paying the Board sums to enable it to meet expenditure of a description specified in the order.

(5) An LHB order may require such a Health Authority or an NHS trust in Wales to make available to the Local Health Board during the preparatory period—

(a) premises and other facilities of the authority or NHS trust;

(b) officers of the authority;

(c) staff of the NHS trust.

PART 2

STATUS, CONSTITUTION AND MEMBERSHIP

Status

3   A Local Health Board is not to be regarded as the servant or agent of the Crown or as enjoying any status, immunity or privilege of the Crown; and a Local Health Board's property is not to be regarded as property of, or property held on behalf of, the Crown.

4   Every Local Health Board shall be a body corporate.

Membership

5   The members of a Local Health Board shall be—

(a) a chairman appointed by the National Assembly for Wales;

(b) if the Assembly thinks fit, a vice-chairman appointed by the Assembly;

(c) officers of the Board; and

(d) a number of persons who are not officers of the Board.

6   (1) The National Assembly for Wales may by regulations make provision about—

    (a) the appointment of the chairman, vice-chairman and other members of a Local Health Board (including any conditions to be fulfilled for appointment);

    (b) the tenure of office of the chairman, vice-chairman and other members of a Local Health Board (including the circumstances in which they cease to hold office or may be removed or suspended from office);

    (c) how many persons may be appointed as members of a Local Health Board and how many of those members may be officers (a minimum and maximum number may be specified for both purposes);

    (d) the appointment and constitution of any committees of a Local Health Board (which may include or consist of persons who are not members of the Board);

    (e) the appointment and tenure of office of the members of any committees of a Local Health Board;

    (f) the procedure to be followed by a Local Health Board, and by any committee of the Board, in the exercise of its functions;

    (g) the circumstances in which a person who is not an officer of the Local Health Board is to be treated as if he were such an officer.

  (2) The power to make provision under paragraphs (c) and (f) of sub-paragraph (1) above includes power to make regulations about the number of persons who may be appointed and the procedure to be followed during the preparatory period.

  (3) Any regulations under this paragraph may, in particular, make provision to deal with cases where the post of any officer of a Local Health Board is held jointly by two or more persons or where the functions of such an officer are in any other way performed by more than one person.

7   Any reference in this Part of this Schedule to a committee of a Local Health Board includes a reference to sub-committees of, and joint committees and joint sub-committees including, the Board.

8   The validity of proceedings of a Local Health Board, or of any of its committees, shall not be affected by any vacancy among the members or by any defect in the appointment of any member.

Staff

9   (1) A Local Health Board may employ such officers as it thinks fit.

  (2) Subject to sub-paragraph (3) below, a Board may—

    (a) pay its officers such remuneration and allowances; and

    (b) employ them on such other terms and conditions,

  as it thinks fit.

  (3) A Board shall—

    (a) in exercising its powers under sub-paragraph (2) above; and

 (b) otherwise in connection with the employment of its officers,

act in accordance with regulations made by the National Assembly for Wales and any directions given by the Assembly.

 (4) Before making any regulations under sub-paragraph (3) above, the Assembly shall consult such bodies as it may recognise as representing persons who, in its opinion, are likely to be affected by the regulations.

10 (1) Without prejudice to the generality of section 16BB above the National Assembly for Wales may direct a Local Health Board –

  (a) to make the services of any of its officers available to another Local Health Board; or

  (b) to employ any person who is or was employed by another Local Health Board and is specified in the direction.

 (2) Before it gives a direction under sub-paragraph (1) above the Assembly shall –

  (a) consult the person whose services are to be made available or who is to be employed;

  (b) satisfy itself that the Board has consulted that person; or

  (c) consult any such body as the Assembly may recognise as representing that person.

 (3) Sub-paragraph (2) above does not apply in relation to a direction under sub-paragraph (1)(a) above if the Assembly –

  (a) considers it necessary to give the direction for the purpose of dealing temporarily with an emergency; and

  (b) has previously consulted bodies recognised by the Assembly as representing the person whose services are to be made available about the giving of directions for that purpose.

11 In addition to making provision in relation to Strategic Health Authorities, Health Authorities and Special Health Authorities, regulations under paragraph 10(2) of Schedule 5 to this Act may also provide –

  (a) for the transfer of officers of one Local Health Board to another; and

  (b) for arrangements under which the officers of a Local Health Board are placed at the disposal of another Local Health Board or a local authority.

Remuneration, pensions etc of members

12 (1) A Local Health Board may pay the chairman, the vice-chairman (if any) and any other members of the Board such remuneration and such travelling and other allowances as may be determined by the National Assembly for Wales.

 (2) A Board may pay the chairman or any person who has been chairman of the Board such pension, allowance or gratuity as may be determined by the National Assembly for Wales.

(3) A Board may pay the members of any committee of a Board such travelling and other allowances as may be determined by the National Assembly for Wales.

(4) If, when a person ceases to be chairman of a Board, the National Assembly for Wales determines that there are special circumstances which make it right that that person should receive compensation, the Board shall pay to him a sum by way of compensation of such amount as the Assembly may determine.

PART 3

OTHER MATTERS

General powers

13 (1) Subject to sub-paragraph (3), a Local Health Board may do anything which appears to it to be necessary or expedient for the purpose of or in connection with the exercise of its functions.

(2) That includes, in particular —

(a) acquiring and disposing of land and other property;

(b) entering into contracts;

(c) accepting gifts of money, land and other property, including money, land or other property held on trust, either for the general or any specific purposes of the Local Health Board or for all or any purposes relating to the health service.

(3) A Local Health Board may not do anything mentioned in sub-paragraph (2) without the consent of the Assembly (which may, if the Assembly thinks fit, be given in general terms covering one or more descriptions of case).

14 (1) Any rights acquired, or liabilities (including liabilities in tort) incurred, in respect of the exercise by a Local Health Board of any function exercisable by it by virtue of section 16BB or 16BC above are enforceable by or (as the case may be) against that Board (and not against any other health service body or the National Assembly for Wales).

(2) This paragraph does not apply in relation to the joint exercise of any functions by a Local Health Board with another body under section 16BC(2)(c) above.

Specific powers and duties

15 (1) A Local Health Board may conduct, commission or assist the conduct of research.

(2) A Board may, in particular, make officers available or provide facilities under sub-paragraph (1) above.

16 A Local Health Board may —

(a) make officers available in connection with any instruction provided under section 63 of the Health Services and Public Health Act 1968;

        (b)   make officers and facilities available in connection with training by a university or any other body providing training in connection with the health service.

17   The National Assembly for Wales may by regulations make provision in relation to —

        (a)   reports to be prepared by Local Health Boards;

        (b)   information to be supplied by them;

        (c)   their accounts, and the audit and publication of their accounts;

        (d)   the publication of any other document.

Compulsory acquisition

18   (1)   A Local Health Board may be authorised to purchase land compulsorily for the purposes of its functions by means of an order made by the Board and confirmed by the National Assembly for Wales.

      (2)   The Acquisition of Land Act 1981 applies to the compulsory purchase of land under this paragraph.

      (3)   No order is to be made by a Local Health Board under Part 2 of the Acquisition of Land Act 1981 in respect of any land unless the proposal to acquire the land compulsorily —

        (a)   has been submitted to the National Assembly for Wales in the form, and with the information, required by the Assembly; and

        (b)   has been approved by the Assembly.

Dissolution

19   (1)   The National Assembly for Wales may, if a Local Health Board is dissolved, by order transfer (or provide for the transfer) to itself or to another Local Health Board any property, rights or liabilities of the dissolved Board.

      (2)   If any consultation requirements apply, they must be complied with before the order is made.

      (3)   In this paragraph, "consultation requirements" means requirements about consultation contained in regulations made by the Assembly.

Transfer of property

20   (1)   The National Assembly for Wales may by order (referred to in this paragraph and paragraph 21 below as a transfer order) —

        (a)   transfer (or provide for the transfer of) any of the property, rights and liabilities of a health service authority to a Local Health Board;

        (b)   create or impose (or provide for the creation or imposition of) new rights or liabilities in respect of property transferred or retained.

      (2)   Any property, rights and liabilities which —

(a) belong to a health service authority other than the National Assembly for Wales or are used or managed by a Health Authority; and

(b) are to be transferred to a Local Health Board by or under a transfer order,

must be identified by agreement between the health service authority (or Health Authority) and the Local Health Board or, in default of agreement, by direction of the Assembly.

(3) Where a transfer order transfers (or provides for the transfer of) —

(a) land held on lease from a third party; or

(b) any other asset leased or hired from a third party or in which a third party has an interest,

the transfer is binding on the third party despite the fact that, apart from this sub-paragraph, the transfer would have required the third party's consent or concurrence.

(4) In sub-paragraph (3) above, "third party" means a person other than a health service authority.

(5) In this paragraph and paragraph 21 below, "health service authority" means the National Assembly for Wales, a Health Authority, a Local Health Board or an NHS trust in Wales.

21 (1) Stamp duty is not chargeable in respect of any transfer to a Local Health Board effected by or under a transfer order.

(2) Where it becomes necessary, for the purpose of a transfer by or under a transfer order, to apportion any property, rights or liabilities, the order may contain such provisions as appear to the National Assembly for Wales to be appropriate for the purpose.

(3) Where a transfer order transfers (or provides for the transfer of) any property or rights to which paragraph 20(3) above applies, the order must contain such provisions as appear to the National Assembly for Wales to be appropriate to safeguard the interests of third parties (within the meaning of that sub-paragraph), including, where appropriate, provision for the payment of compensation of an amount to be determined in accordance with the order.

(4) A certificate issued by the National Assembly for Wales that —

(a) any specified property;

(b) any specified interest in or right over any property; or

(c) any specified right or liability,

has been vested in a Local Health Board by or under a transfer order is conclusive evidence of that fact for all purposes.

In this sub-paragraph, "specified" means specified in the certificate.

(5) A transfer order may include provision for matters to be settled by arbitration by a person determined in accordance with the order.

(6) Paragraph 20 above and this paragraph do not prejudice —

(a) any existing power of a health service authority to transfer property, rights or liabilities to a Local Health Board;

(b) the extent of the power conferred by section 126(4) above.

Transfer of staff

22 (1) The National Assembly for Wales may by order transfer to a Local Health Board any specified description of employees to which this paragraph applies.

(2) This paragraph applies to employees of —
    (a) a Health Authority;
    (b) an NHS trust in Wales;
    (c) a Local Health Board.

(3) An order may be made under this paragraph only if any prescribed requirements about consultation have been complied with in relation to each of the employees to be transferred.

23 (1) The contract of employment of an employee transferred under paragraph 22 above —
    (a) is not terminated by the transfer; and
    (b) has effect from the date of the transfer as if originally made between the employee and the Local Health Board to which he is transferred.

(2) Without prejudice to sub-paragraph (1) above —
    (a) all the rights, powers, duties and liabilities of the body from which an employee is transferred under paragraph 22 above under or in connection with his contract of employment shall by virtue of this sub-paragraph be transferred to the Local Health Board to which the employee is transferred under that paragraph; and
    (b) anything done before the date of the transfer by or in relation to the body from which he is so transferred in respect of the employee or the contract of employment shall be deemed from that date to have been done by or in relation to the Local Health Board to which he is transferred.

(3) Sub-paragraphs (1) and (2) above do not transfer an employee's contract of employment, or the rights, powers, duties and liabilities under or in connection with it, if he informs the body from which they would be transferred, or the Local Health Board to which they would be transferred, that he objects to the transfer.

(4) Where an employee objects as mentioned in sub-paragraph (3) above his contract of employment with the body from which he would be transferred shall be terminated immediately before the date on which the transfer would occur; but he shall not be treated, for any purpose, as having been dismissed by that body.

(5) This paragraph is without prejudice to any right of an employee to which paragraph 22 above applies to terminate his contract of employment if a substantial change is made to his detriment in his working conditions; but no such right shall arise merely because, under this paragraph, the identity of his employer changes unless the employee shows that, in all the circumstances, the change is a significant change and is to his detriment.

24 (1) Where an employee is to be transferred by an order under paragraph 22 above but is to continue to be employed for certain purposes by the transferor, the order may provide that the

contract of employment of the employee shall, on the date on which the employee is transferred, be divided so as to constitute two separate contracts of employment between the employee and the transferor and the employee and the Local Health Board in question.

(2) Where an employee's contract of employment is divided as provided under sub-paragraph (1) above, the order shall provide for paragraph 23 above to have effect in the case of the employee and his contract of employment subject to appropriate modifications.

25   Where a Local Health Board is dissolved, an order under paragraph 19 above includes power to transfer employees of the Board and the order may make any provision in relation to the transfer of those employees which is or may be made in relation to the transfer of employees under paragraph 22 above.

Interpretation

26   In this Schedule, "NHS trust in Wales" means an NHS trust all or most of whose hospitals, establishments and facilities are situated in Wales."

SCHEDULE 5 Section 6(2)

AMENDMENTS RELATING TO LOCAL HEALTH BOARDS

The Public Bodies (Admission to Meetings) Act 1960 (c. 67)

1   In the Schedule to the Public Bodies (Admission to Meetings) Act 1960 (bodies to which the Act applies), after paragraph 1(gg) there is inserted —
        "(gh)   Local Health Boards;".

The Health Services and Public Health Act 1968 (c. 46)

2   (1) Section 63 of the Health Services and Public Health Act 1968 (provision of instruction for officers of hospital authorities etc) is amended as follows.

(2) In subsection (1)(a), for "or Primary Care Trust" there is substituted ", Primary Care Trust or Local Health Board".

(3) In subsection (5A), for "or Primary Care Trust", in both places, there is substituted ", Primary Care Trust or Local Health Board".

(4) In subsection (5B), the "and" at the end of paragraph (bb) is omitted, and after that paragraph there is inserted —
        "(bbb)   Local Health Boards; and".

The Employers' Liability (Compulsory Insurance) Act 1969 (c. 57)

3   In section 3 of the Employers' Liability (Compulsory Insurance) Act 1969 (employers exempted from insurance), in subsection (2)(a) —
        (a)   for "1978 and" there is substituted "1978,", and

       (b)   after "1977" there is inserted "and a Local Health Board established under section 16BA of that Act".

The 1977 Act

4   The 1977 Act is amended as follows.

5   In section 16 (exercise of functions), in subsection (2)(c), after "Trusts" there is inserted ", Local Health Boards".

6   In section 16B (exercise of functions by Primary Care Trusts), in subsection (2)(c), after "NHS trusts" there is inserted ", Local Health Boards".

7   In section 16C (advice for Health Authorities and Primary Care Trusts), in subsection (2), after "Primary Care Trusts" there is inserted "and Local Health Boards".

8   In section 22 (co-operation between health authorities and local authorities), in subsection (1A), the "or" at the end of paragraph (c) is omitted and after that paragraph there is inserted —

          "(cc)   a Local Health Board; or".

9   In section 23 (voluntary organisations and other bodies), in subsection (2), for "or Primary Care Trust" there is substituted ", Primary Care Trust or Local Health Board".

10   In section 26 (supply of goods and services by Secretary of State), in subsection (1)(b), for "or Primary Care Trust" there is substituted ", Primary Care Trust or Local Health Board".

11   In section 27 (conditions of supply under section 26) —

       (a)   in subsection (1), for "or Primary Care Trust", in both places, there is substituted ", Primary Care Trust or Local Health Board", and

       (b)   in subsection (3), for "and Primary Care Trusts" there is substituted ", Primary Care Trusts and Local Health Boards".

12   In section 28 (supply of goods and services by local authorities) —

       (a)   in subsection (1), for "or Primary Care Trust" there is substituted ", Primary Care Trust or Local Health Board", and

       (b)   in subsection (3), after "Primary Care Trusts", in both places, there is inserted ", Local Health Boards".

13   In section 28A (power to make payments towards expenditure on community services) —

       (a)   in subsection (1) —

           (i)   the "and" at the end of paragraph (a) is omitted, and

           (ii)   at the end of paragraph (b) there is inserted "; and", and after that paragraph there is inserted —

                "(c)   a Local Health Board.", and

       (b)   in subsection (2B), after "Primary Care Trust" there is inserted ", Local Health Board".

14   In section 28BB (power of local authorities to make payments to NHS bodies), in subsection (2), in the definition of "relevant NHS body", after "Primary Care Trust" there is inserted "or Local Health Board".

15   In section 51 (university clinical teaching and research) —

National Health Service Reform and Health Care Professions Act 2002 (c. 17)
Schedule 5 — Amendments relating to Local Health Boards

83

      (a)   in subsection (2), for "or Primary Care Trust", in both places, there is substituted ", Primary Care Trust or Local Health Board", and

      (b)   in subsection (3), the "and" at the end of paragraph (bb) is omitted and after that paragraph there is inserted —

          "(bbb)   Local Health Boards; and".

16   In section 84A (intervention orders), in subsection (2), after paragraph (d) there is inserted —

          "(e)   Local Health Boards."

17   In section 84B (intervention orders: effect), in subsection (1), in each of paragraphs (a) and (b), for "or Primary Care Trust" there is substituted ", Primary Care Trust or Local Health Board".

18   In section 85 (Secretary of State's default powers), in subsection (1), after paragraph (bb) there is inserted —

          "(bbb)   a Local Health Board;".

19   In section 92 (further transfers of trust property), in subsection (1A), after paragraph (c) there is inserted —

          "(cc)   a Local Health Board;".

20   In section 96A (power of health authorities etc to raise money), in each of subsections (1), (3), (4), (7), (8) and (9), after "Special Health Authority", in each place where it occurs, there is inserted ", Local Health Board".

21   In section 98 (accounts and audit), in subsection (1), after paragraph (bb) there is inserted —

          "(bbb)   every Local Health Board;".

22   In section 99 (regulation of financial arrangements), in subsection (1), after paragraph (ba) there is inserted —

          "(bb)   Local Health Boards;".

23   In section 125 (protection of members and officers of authorities), the "and" at the end of paragraph (bb) is omitted and after that paragraph there is inserted —

          "(bbb)   a Local Health Board; and".

24   In paragraph 2 of Schedule 7 (which makes additional provision in relation to Community Health Councils) —

      (a)   in sub-paragraphs (d) and (e), after "Primary Care Trusts", in each place where it occurs, there is inserted ", Local Health Boards", and

      (b)   in sub-paragraphs (f) and (g), for "and Primary Care Trusts" there is substituted ", Primary Care Trusts and Local Health Boards".

The Acquisition of Land Act 1981 (c. 67)

25   In section 16 of the Acquisition of Land Act 1981 (statutory undertakers' land excluded from compulsory purchase), in subsection (3), the "and" at the end of paragraph (b) is omitted, and at the end of paragraph (c) there is inserted "and

          (d)   a Local Health Board established under section 16BA of that Act;".

The Hospital Complaints Procedure Act 1985 (c. 42)

26   In section 1 of the Hospital Complaints Procedure Act 1985 (hospital
complaints procedure), in subsection (1B), after "Trust", where it first occurs,
there is inserted "and Local Health Board", and in the second place where it
occurs there is inserted "or Local Health Board".

The Income and Corporation Taxes Act 1988 (c. 1)

27   In section 519A of the Income and Corporation Taxes Act 1988 (health
service bodies), in subsection (2), after paragraph (ab) there is inserted—
"(aba)   a Local Health Board;".

The Housing Act 1988 (c. 50)

28   In Schedule 2 to the Housing Act 1988 (grounds for possession of dwelling-
houses let on assured tenancies), in the second paragraph of Ground 16, after
"1990," there is inserted "or by a Local Health Board,".

The Road Traffic Act 1988 (c. 52)

29   In section 144 of the Road Traffic Act 1988 (exceptions from requirement of
third-party insurance or security), in subsection (2)(da), after "1977" there is
inserted ", by a Local Health Board established under section 16BA of that
Act".

The National Health Service and Community Care Act 1990 (c. 19)

30   The National Health Service and Community Care Act 1990 is amended as
follows.

31   In section 4 (NHS contracts), in subsection (2), after paragraph (bb) there is
inserted—
"(bbb)   a Local Health Board;".

32   In section 8 (transfer of property, rights and liabilities to NHS trust)—
(a)   in subsections (1), (2), (3) and (5), for "or Primary Care Trust" there is
substituted ", Primary Care Trust or Local Health Board", and
(b)   in subsection (6)—
(i)   in paragraph (a), after "Health Authority" there is inserted
", Local Health Board", and
(ii)   for "or Primary Care Trust" there is substituted ", Primary
Care Trust or Local Health Board".

33   In section 21 (schemes for meeting losses and liabilities of certain health
service bodies), in subsection (2), after paragraph (aaa) there is inserted—
"(aab)   Local Health Boards;".

34   In section 49 (transfer of staff from health service to local authorities), in
subsection (4)(b), after "Health Authority" there is inserted ", Local Health
Board".

35   In section 61 (health service bodies: taxation), in subsection (3), after
"Primary Care Trust" there is inserted "or Local Health Board".

National Health Service Reform and Health Care Professions Act 2002 (c. 17)
Schedule 5 – Amendments relating to Local Health Boards

85

36 (1) Schedule 2 (National Health Service trusts) is amended as provided in this paragraph.

(2) In paragraph 4, for "or Primary Care Trust", in both places, there is substituted ", Primary Care Trust or Local Health Board".

(3) In paragraph 13, after "Primary Care Trust" there is inserted "or Local Health Board".

(4) In paragraph 30(1), after paragraph (bbb) there is inserted —

"(bbc) a Local Health Board, or".

The Welsh Language Act 1993 (c. 38)

37 In section 6 of the Welsh Language Act 1993 (meaning of "public body"), in subsection (1), after paragraph (f) there is inserted —

"(ff) a Local Health Board established under section 16BA of the National Health Service Act 1977;".

The Health Service Commissioners Act 1993 (c. 46)

38 In the Health Service Commissioners Act 1993, in section 2 (bodies subject to investigation), in subsection (2), for paragraph (aa) there is substituted —

"(aa) Local Health Boards,".

The Vehicle Excise and Registration Act 1994 (c. 22)

39 In Schedule 2 to the Vehicle Excise and Registration Act 1994 (exempt vehicles), in paragraph 7, at the end of sub-paragraph (d) there is inserted "or

(e) a Local Health Board established under section 16BA of that Act."

The Value Added Tax Act 1994 (c. 23)

40 In section 41 of the Value Added Tax Act 1994 (application to Crown), in subsection (7), after "Primary Care Trust" there is inserted "and a Local Health Board".

The Data Protection Act 1998 (c. 29)

41 In section 69 of the Data Protection Act 1998 (meaning of "health professional"), in subsection (3), after paragraph (bb) there is inserted —

"(bbb) a Local Health Board established under section 16BA of that Act,".

The Government of Wales Act 1998 (c. 38)

42 (1) The Government of Wales Act 1998 is amended as provided in this paragraph.

(2) In Schedule 5 (bodies and offices covered by section 74), after paragraph 25 there is inserted —

"25A. A Local Health Board."

(3) In Schedule 17 (audit etc of Welsh public bodies), after paragraph 12 there is inserted −

"12A.   A Local Health Board."

The 1999 Act

43   The 1999 Act is amended as follows.

44   In section 20 (functions of the Commission for Health Improvement), after subsection (7) there is inserted −

"(8)   If a Local Health Board has responsibility for any health care −

(a)   paragraphs (a), (b) and (c) of subsection (1) are to be read as if they included a reference to that Local Health Board as well as to the bodies which are mentioned there, and

(b)   the definition of "NHS body" in subsection (7) is to be read as if it included a reference to that Local Health Board."

45   In section 31 (arrangements between NHS bodies and local authorities), in subsection (8), in the definition of "NHS body", after "Primary Care Trust" there is inserted ", Local Health Board".

The Care Standards Act 2000 (c. 14)

46   In section 121 of the Care Standards Act 2000 (general interpretation), in subsection (1), in the definition of "National Health Service body", for "or a Primary Care Trust" there is substituted ", a Primary Care Trust or a Local Health Board".

The Learning and Skills Act 2000 (c. 21)

47   In section 138 of the Learning and Skills Act 2000 (Wales: provision of information by public bodies), in subsection (3), after paragraph (b) there is inserted −

"(ba)   a Local Health Board,".

The Freedom of Information Act 2000 (c. 36)

48   In Schedule 1 to the Freedom of Information Act 2000 (public authorities for the purposes of the Act), in Part 3 (National Health Service), after paragraph 39 there is inserted −

"39A.   A Local Health Board established under section 16BA of the National Health Service Act 1977."

The Health and Social Care Act 2001 (c. 15)

49   The Health and Social Care Act 2001 is amended as follows.

50   In section 7 (functions of overview and scrutiny committees), in subsection (4), after "Primary Care Trust" there is inserted ", Local Health Board".

51   In section 46 (directed partnership arrangements), in subsection (5), in the definition of "NHS body", after "Primary Care Trust" there is inserted ", Local Health Board".

National Health Service Reform and Health Care Professions Act 2002 (c. 17)
Schedule 6 – The Commission for Patient and Public Involvement in Health

87

SCHEDULE 6   Section 20(11)

THE COMMISSION FOR PATIENT AND PUBLIC INVOLVEMENT IN HEALTH

Status

1   The Commission for Patient and Public Involvement in Health ("the Commission") is not to be regarded as the servant or agent of the Crown or as enjoying any status, immunity or privilege of the Crown; and the Commission's property is not to be regarded as property of, or property held on behalf of, the Crown.

Powers

2   (1) Subject to any directions given by the Secretary of State, the Commission may do anything which appears to it to be necessary or expedient for the purposes of, or in connection with, the exercise of its functions.

     (2) That includes, in particular –
         (a) acquiring and disposing of land and other property, and
         (b) entering into contracts.

Membership

3   The Commission is to consist of a chairman appointed by the Secretary of State, and a number of other members.

Appointment, procedure etc

4   (1) The Secretary of State may by regulations make provision as to –
         (a) the appointment of the chairman and other members of the Commission (including the number, or limits on the number, of members who may be appointed and any conditions to be fulfilled for appointment, and the terms of their appointment),
         (b) the tenure of office of the chairman and other members of the Commission (including circumstances in which they cease to hold office or may be removed or suspended from office),
         (c) the appointment of, constitution of and exercise of functions by committees and sub-committees of the Commission (including committees and sub-committees which consist of or include persons who are not members of the Commission),
         (d) the procedure of the Commission and any of its committees or sub-committees (including the validation of proceedings in the event of vacancies or defects in appointment).

     (2) The regulations may, in particular, make provision to deal with cases where the post of any officer of the Commission is held jointly by two or more persons or where the functions of such an officer are in any other way performed by more than one person.

5   The regulations may include provision applying, or corresponding to, any provision of Part 5A of the Local Government Act 1972 (access to meetings and documents), with or without modifications.

6   (1) The Secretary of State may direct a Special Health Authority to exercise –
         (a) his function of appointing the chairman under paragraph 3, and

     (b)   any functions conferred on him by regulations made under paragraph 4 in relation to the appointment or the tenure of office of the chairman and the other members.

(2) If he does so, the 1977 Act has effect as if —

     (a)   the directions were directions of the Secretary of State under section 16D of that Act, and, accordingly,

     (b)   the functions were exercisable by the Special Health Authority under section 16D.

Remuneration and allowances

7   (1) The Commission may pay to its chairman and to any other member such remuneration and allowances as the Secretary of State may determine.

    (2) The Commission may pay to any member of a committee or sub-committee such allowances as the Secretary of State may determine.

    (3) If the Secretary of State so determines, the Commission must pay, or make provision for the payment of, such pension, allowance or gratuities as the Secretary of State may determine to or in respect of a person who is or has been the chairman or any other member of the Commission.

    (4) If the Secretary of State determines that there are special circumstances that make it right for a person ceasing to hold office as chairman of the Commission to receive compensation, the Commission must pay to him such compensation as the Secretary of State may determine.

Staff

8   (1) There is to be a Chief Executive of the Commission who is to be an employee of the Commission and is to be responsible to the Commission for the general exercise of the Commission's functions.

    (2) Subject to sub-paragraph (3), the Chief Executive is to be appointed by the Commission.

    (3) The first Chief Executive is to be appointed by the Secretary of State on such terms and conditions as the Secretary of State may determine.

    (4) The Commission may appoint such other employees as it considers appropriate, on such terms and conditions as the Commission may determine.

Delegation of functions

9   The Commission may arrange for the discharge of any of its functions by a committee, sub-committee, member or employee of the Commission.

Assistance

10 (1) The Commission may arrange for such persons as it thinks fit to assist it in the discharge of any of its functions.

    (2) Such arrangements may include provision with respect to the payment of remuneration and allowances to, or amounts in respect of, such persons.

National Health Service Reform and Health Care Professions Act 2002 (c. 17)
Schedule 6 – The Commission for Patient and Public Involvement in Health

89

Payments and loans to the Commission

11 (1) The Secretary of State may make payments out of money provided by Parliament to the Commission of such amounts, at such times and on such conditions (if any) as he considers appropriate.

(2) The Secretary of State may make loans out of money provided by Parliament to the Commission on such terms (including terms as to repayment and interest) as he may determine.

(3) The approval of the Treasury is required as to the amount and terms of any loan under sub-paragraph (2).

(4) The Secretary of State may give directions to the Commission as to the application of any sums he pays it under sub-paragraph (1) or (2), and the Commission must comply with any such directions.

Accounts and audit

12 (1) The Commission must keep accounts in such form as the Secretary of State may determine.

(2) The Commission must prepare annual accounts in respect of each financial year in such form as the Secretary of State may determine.

(3) The Commission must send copies of the annual accounts to the Secretary of State and the Comptroller and Auditor General within such period after the end of the financial year to which the accounts relate as the Secretary of State may determine.

(4) The Comptroller and Auditor General must examine, certify and report on the annual accounts and must lay copies of the accounts and of his report before Parliament.

(5) In this paragraph, "financial year" means —
(a) the period beginning with the date on which the Commission is established and ending with the next 31st March, and
(b) each successive period of 12 months ending with 31st March.

Reports and other information

13 (1) The Commission shall —
(a) prepare a report in relation to its activities in each financial year,
(b) as soon as possible after the end of each financial year, send a copy of its report for that year to the Secretary of State,
(c) publish any such report in whichever way the Commission considers appropriate,
(d) make such other reports to the Secretary of State, and supply to him such information, as he may require.

(2) The Secretary of State shall lay before Parliament any report he receives under sub-paragraph (1)(b).

(3) The Secretary of State may make regulations providing for the Commission to make other reports, in accordance with the regulations, to prescribed persons or descriptions of person.

(4) In this paragraph "financial year" has the meaning given in paragraph 12(5).

Application of seal and evidence

14   The application of the seal of the Commission must be authenticated by the signature —

         (a)   of any member of the Commission, or

         (b)   of any other person who has been authorised by the Commission (whether generally or specially) for that purpose.

15   A document purporting to be duly executed under the seal of the Commission or to be signed on its behalf is to be received in evidence and, unless the contrary is proved, taken to be so executed or signed.

Miscellaneous amendments

16   In the First Schedule to the Public Records Act 1958 (c. 51) (definition of public records), the following entry is inserted at the appropriate place in Part 2 of the Table at the end of paragraph 3 —

     "Commission for Patient and Public Involvement in Health."

17   In Schedule 2 to the Parliamentary Commissioner Act 1967 (c. 13) (departments etc subject to investigation), the following entry is inserted at the appropriate place —

     "Commission for Patient and Public Involvement in Health."

18   In Part 2 of Schedule 1 to the House of Commons Disqualification Act 1975 (c. 24) (bodies of which all members are disqualified), the following entry is inserted at the appropriate place —

     "The Commission for Patient and Public Involvement in Health."

19   In Schedule 1 to the Freedom of Information Act 2000 (c. 36) (public authorities for the purposes of the Act), in Part 3 (National Health Service), after paragraph 45A there is inserted —

     "45B   The Commission for Patient and Public Involvement in Health."

SCHEDULE 7   Section 25(4)

THE COUNCIL FOR THE REGULATION OF HEALTH CARE PROFESSIONALS

Status

1   The Council is not to be regarded as the servant or agent of the Crown or as enjoying any status, immunity or privilege of the Crown; and the Council's property is not to be regarded as property of, or property held on behalf of, the Crown.

2   For the purposes of —

         (a)   section 23(2)(b) of the Scotland Act 1998 (c. 46) (power of Scottish Parliament to require persons outside Scotland to attend to give evidence or produce documents); and

         (b)   section 70(6) of that Act (accounts prepared by cross-border bodies),

     the Council is to be treated as a cross-border public authority within the meaning of that Act.

National Health Service Reform and Health Care Professions Act 2002 (c. 17)
Schedule 7 – The Council for the Regulation of Health Care Professionals

91

Powers

3   The power in section 26(1) includes the power to —
    (a)   acquire and dispose of land and other property, and
    (b)   enter into contracts.

Membership and chairman

4   (1) The Council is to consist of —
    (a)   a member appointed by the National Assembly for Wales,
    (b)   a member appointed by the Scottish Ministers,
    (c)   a member appointed by the Department of Health, Social Services and Public Safety in Northern Ireland,
    (d)   a member appointed by each regulatory body (who need not be a member of a regulatory body), and
    (e)   other members appointed by the Secretary of State.

    (2) Subject to sub-paragraph (3), the members of the Council shall elect one of their number as chairman.

    (3) The first chairman shall be appointed as such from among the members by the Secretary of State.

    (4) The number of members to be appointed under paragraph (d) of sub-paragraph (1) is to be one fewer than the total number of other members.

Appointment, procedure etc

5   (1) The Secretary of State may direct a Special Health Authority to exercise his function of appointing members of the Council under paragraph 4(1)(e).

    (2) If he does so, the 1977 Act has effect as if —
    (a)   the directions were directions of the Secretary of State under section 16D of that Act, and, accordingly,
    (b)   the function were exercisable by the Special Health Authority under section 16D.

6   The Secretary of State may by regulations provide for —
    (a)   the election of the chairman and the appointment of other members of the Council (including any conditions to be fulfilled for appointment),
    (b)   the tenure of office of the chairman and other members of the Council (including the circumstances in which they cease to hold office or may be removed or suspended from office), and
    (c)   the appointment of, constitution of and exercise of functions by committees and sub-committees of the Council (including committees and sub-committees which consist of or include persons who are not members of the Council).

7   The Council may regulate its own procedure.

8   The validity of any proceedings of the Council is not affected by a vacancy amongst its members or by a defect in the appointment of a member.

Members' interests

9   (1) The Council must establish and maintain a system for the declaration and
         registration of private interests of its members.

     (2) The Council must publish entries recorded in the register of members'
         interests.

Remuneration and allowances

10   (1) The Council may pay to its chairman, and to any other member of the
         Council, such remuneration and allowances as the Secretary of State may
         determine.

     (2) The Council may pay to any member of a committee or sub-committee of the
         Council such allowances as the Secretary of State may determine.

     (3) If the Secretary of State so determines, the Council must provide for the
         payment of such pension, allowance or gratuities as the Secretary of State
         may determine to or in respect of a person who is or has been the chairman
         or any other member of the Council.

     (4) If the Secretary of State determines that there are special circumstances that
         make it right for a person ceasing to hold office as chairman of the Council
         to receive compensation, the Council must pay to him such compensation as
         the Secretary of State may determine.

Employees

11   The Council may appoint such employees as it considers appropriate on
         such terms and conditions as it may determine.

Delegation of functions

12   (1) The Council may arrange for the discharge of any of its functions by —
         (a)   a committee, sub-committee, member or employee of the Council, or
         (b)   any other person.

     (2) If the Council does arrange for the discharge of any function as mentioned
         in sub-paragraph (1)(b), the arrangements may include provision with
         respect to the payment of remuneration and allowances to, or amounts in
         respect of, such persons.

Assistance

13   (1) The Council may arrange for such persons as it thinks fit to assist it in the
         discharge of any of its functions in relation to a particular case or class of
         case.

     (2) Such arrangements may include provision with respect to the payment of
         remuneration and allowances to, or amounts in respect of, such persons.

Payments and loans to Council

14   (1) The Secretary of State may make payments out of money provided by
         Parliament to the Council of such amounts, at such times and on such
         conditions (if any) as he considers appropriate.

(2) An appropriate authority may make payments to the Council of such amounts, at such times and on such conditions (if any) as it considers appropriate.

(3) The Secretary of State may make loans out of money provided by Parliament to the Council on such terms (including terms as to repayment and interest) as he may determine.

(4) An appropriate authority may make loans to the Council on such terms (including terms as to repayment and interest) as it may determine.

(5) The approval of the Treasury is required as to the amount and terms of any loan under sub-paragraph (3).

(6) Except as provided by sub-paragraphs (3) and (4), the Council has no power to borrow money.

(7) The Secretary of State may give directions to the Council as to the application of any sums received by it under sub-paragraph (1) or (3).

(8) An appropriate authority may give directions to the Council as to the application of any sums received by it from the authority under sub-paragraph (2) or (4).

(9) The Council must comply with any directions under sub-paragraph (7) or (8).

(10) In this paragraph, "appropriate authority" means the National Assembly for Wales, the Scottish Ministers or the Department of Health, Social Services and Public Safety in Northern Ireland.

Accounts

15 (1) The Council must keep accounts in such form as the Secretary of State may determine.

(2) The Council must prepare annual accounts in respect of each financial year in such form as the Secretary of State may determine.

(3) The Council must send copies of the annual accounts to the Secretary of State and the Comptroller and Auditor General within such period after the end of the financial year to which the accounts relate as the Secretary of State may determine.

(4) Within that period the Council must also send copies of the annual accounts to —
   (a)   the Scottish Ministers,
   (b)   the National Assembly for Wales, and
   (c)   the Department of Health, Social Services and Public Safety in Northern Ireland.

(5) The Comptroller and Auditor General must examine, certify and report on the annual accounts and must lay copies of the accounts and of his report before Parliament.

(6) A copy of the accounts shall be laid before —
   (a)   the Scottish Parliament by the Scottish Ministers,
   (b)   the Northern Ireland Assembly by the Department of Health, Social Services and Public Safety there,
   and the National Assembly for Wales shall publish the accounts.

(7) In this paragraph and paragraph 16, "financial year" means —

(a)   the period beginning with the date on which the Council is established and ending with the next 31st March following that date, and

(b)   each successive period of 12 months ending with 31st March.

Reports and other information

16   (1)   The Council must prepare a report on the exercise of its functions during each financial year.

(2)   As soon as possible after the end of each financial year, the Council must lay a copy of its report for that year before Parliament, the Scottish Parliament, the National Assembly for Wales and the Northern Ireland Assembly.

(3)   The Council must comply with any request by Parliament to prepare, and lay before it, other reports or to provide Parliament with other information.

(4)   The Council must also comply with any corresponding request by –

(a)   the Scottish Parliament, in relation to matters which concern a subject for which any member of the Scottish Executive has general responsibility,

(b)   the Northern Ireland Assembly, in relation to transferred matters concerning Northern Ireland ("transferred matters" having the meaning given by section 4(1) of the Northern Ireland Act 1998 (c. 47)).

Application of seal and evidence

17   The application of the seal of the Council must be authenticated by the signature of –

(a)   any member of the Council, or

(b)   any other person who has been authorised by the Council (whether generally or specially) for that purpose.

18   A document purporting to be duly executed under the seal of the Council or to be signed on its behalf is to be received in evidence and, unless the contrary is proved, taken to be so executed or signed.

Meetings of the Council in Northern Ireland

19   (1)   Sections 23 to 27 of the Local Government Act (Northern Ireland) 1972 (c.9) (which provides for public access to meetings of a district council and for the publication of information concerning such meetings) shall, with the modifications set out below, apply in relation to meetings of the Council in Northern Ireland as they apply in relation to meetings of a district council.

(2)   The modifications are –

(a)   any reference to a district council shall be read as a reference to the Council, and

(b)   any reference to councillors or members of the council shall be read as references to members of the Council.

Miscellaneous amendments

20   In the First Schedule to the Public Records Act 1958 (c. 51) (definition of public records), the following entry is inserted at the appropriate place in Part 2 of the Table at the end of paragraph 3 –

"Council for the Regulation of Health Care Professionals.".

21 In the Schedule to the Public Bodies (Admission to Meetings) Act 1960 (c. 67) (bodies to which the Act applies), after paragraph 1(bc) there is inserted —

"(bd) the Council for the Regulation of Health Care Professionals;"

22 In Part 2 of Schedule 1 to the House of Commons Disqualification Act 1975 (c. 24) (bodies of which all members are disqualified), the following entry is inserted at the appropriate place —

"The Council for the Regulation of Health Care Professionals."

23 In Part 2 of Schedule 1 to the Northern Ireland Assembly Disqualification Act 1975 (c. 25) (bodies of which all members are disqualified), the following entry is inserted at the appropriate place —

"The Council for the Regulation of Health Care Professionals."

24 In Part 6 of Schedule 1 to the Freedom of Information Act 2000 (c. 36) (public bodies and offices: general), the following entry is inserted at the appropriate place —

"The Council for the Regulation of Health Care Professionals."

SCHEDULE 8

Section 37(1)

MINOR AND CONSEQUENTIAL AMENDMENTS

The 1977 Act

1 The 1977 Act is amended as follows.

2 In section 29 (arrangements and regulations for general medical services), in subsection (8), for paragraph (c) there is substituted —

"(c) by an interim suspension order under section 41A of that Act,".

3 In section 43C (indemnity cover), in subsection (3), for the definition of "list" there is substituted —

" "list" means a list of any kind mentioned in paragraphs (a) to (e) of section 49F below;".

4 (1) Section 97A (financial duties of Health Authorities and Special Health Authorities) is amended as follows.

(2) In subsection (1) —

   (a) after "duty of" there is inserted "every Strategic Health Authority and of",

   (b) for "the Health Authority" there is substituted "the Authority", and

   (c) in paragraph (a), after "subsection" there is inserted "(A1) or".

(3) In each of subsections (3), (6), (7) and (8), before "Health Authority", in each place where it occurs, there is inserted "Strategic Health Authority,".

(4) In subsection (9) —

   (a) in paragraph (a), and in the words following paragraph (c), before "Health Authority" there is inserted "Strategic Health Authority,", and

      (b)   in each of paragraphs (b)(i) and (c)(i), before "Health Authority" there is inserted "Strategic Health Authority or".

5   In section 97AA (resource limits for Health Authorities and Special Health Authorities) —

      (a)   in subsection (1), after "duty of" there is inserted "every Strategic Health Authority,", and

      (b)   in subsection (3)(b), before "Health Authority" there is inserted "Strategic Health Authority,".

6   In section 97D (financial duties of Primary Care Trusts), in subsection (1)(b), ", apart from subsection (5A)" is omitted.

7   (1)   Section 97E (resource limits for Primary Care Trusts) is amended as follows.

    (2)   In subsection (1), for "the Health Authority for the trust's area" there is substituted "the Secretary of State".

    (3)   For subsection (2A) there is substituted —

"(2A)   But in specifying an amount for a Primary Care Trust under subsection (1) above (or in varying the amount under subsection (4) below), the Secretary of State may take into account (in whatever way he thinks appropriate) —

      (a)   any such use of resources; and

      (b)   the use of any resources which would have been for the purpose of the trust's general Part 2 expenditure but for an order under section 103(1) below,

during any period he thinks appropriate (or such elements of such uses of resources as he thinks appropriate)."

8   In section 104 (superannuation of officers of certain hospitals), in subsection (1)(a), for "Health Authorities" there is substituted "NHS trusts".

9   In section 105 (payments for certain medical examinations), in subsection (2)(b), after "officer of a" there is inserted "NHS trust, Primary Care Trust,".

10   In section 126 (orders, regulations and directions) —

      (a)   in subsection (4), after "section 16BB, 18" (substituted by section 6(3) of this Act), there is inserted "or 19A(7)", and

      (b)   in subsection (4A), for "directions given in accordance with section 18 above as" there is substituted "the directions".

11   In Schedule 7 (additional provisions about Community Health Councils), in paragraph 7, for the definition of "local authority" there is substituted —

    " "local authority" means the council of a Welsh county or county borough, and".

12   In Schedule 12A (expenditure of Health Authorities and Primary Care Trusts), in each of paragraphs 4(2)(b) and 5(2)(b), for "the Health Authority within whose area the area of the trust falls" there is substituted "the trust".

The Medical Act 1983 (c. 54)

13   The Medical Act 1983 is amended as follows.

National Health Service Reform and Health Care Professions Act 2002 (c. 17)
Schedule 8 – Minor and consequential amendments

97

14   In section 40 (appeals), in subsection (11), for "enabling directions to be given as to the costs of" there is substituted "any order as to costs (or, in Scotland, expenses) in relation to".

15   In Schedule 6 (transitional and saving provisions), in paragraph 18, "section 40(4) of this Act or" is omitted.

The Dentists Act 1984 (c. 24)

16   In section 29 of the Dentists Act 1984 (appeals), in subsection (4), for "enabling directions to be given as to the costs of" there is substituted "any order as to costs (or, in Scotland, expenses) in relation to".

The Opticians Act 1989 (c. 44)

17   In section 23 of the Opticians Act 1989 (appeals in disciplinary and other cases), in subsection (2), for "enabling directions to be given as to the costs of" there is substituted "any order as to costs (or, in Scotland, expenses) in relation to".

The National Health Service and Community Care Act 1990 (c. 19)

18   In section 12 of the National Health Service and Community Care Act 1990 (which relates to functions of health authorities), in subsection (4), the words after paragraph (b) are omitted.

The Local Government (Wales) Act 1994 (c. 19)

19   In Schedule 10 to the Local Government (Wales) Act 1994 (amendments relating to social services), paragraph 11(4) is omitted.

The Health Authorities Act 1995 (c. 17)

20   The Health Authorities Act 1995 is amended as follows.

21   Section 1 (which substituted section 8 of the 1977 Act) is omitted.

22   In Schedule 1 (amendments), paragraphs 32(b), 53 and 107(12)(b) are omitted.

The National Health Service (Primary Care) Act 1997 (c. 46)

23   The National Health Service (Primary Care) Act 1997 is amended as follows.

24   In Part 2 of Schedule 2 (which makes pre-consolidation amendments), paragraphs 71(3), 73 and 75 are omitted.

The Government of Wales Act 1998 (c. 38)

25   The Government of Wales Act 1998 is amended as follows.

26   In section 27 (reform of Welsh health authorities), in subsection (7)(a), for "section 8(1) and (5)(a)" there is substituted "section 8(1)(b) and (5)(b)".

27   Section 148 (Health Authorities) is omitted.

The 1999 Act

28   The 1999 Act is amended as follows.

29   In section 18 (duty of quality), in subsection (1), at the beginning there is inserted "It is the duty of each Strategic Health Authority to put and keep in place arrangements for the purpose of monitoring and improving the quality of health care which is provided to individuals in their area, and".

30   In section 21 (arrangements with the Audit Commission), in subsection (1)(a), for "20(1)(b) or (d)" there is substituted "20(1)(b), (d), (da) or (db)".

31   In Schedule 4 (minor amendments), paragraphs 5, 31(2) and 35 are omitted.

The Health and Social Care Act 2001 (c. 15)

32   The Health and Social Care Act 2001 is amended as follows.

33   In section 1 (determination of allotments to and resource limits for Health Authorities and Primary Care Trusts), subsections (4) and (5) are omitted.

34   In section 3 (supplementary payments to NHS trusts and Primary Care Trusts), subsections (3) and (4) are omitted.

35   In section 11 (public involvement and consultation) —
            (a)   in subsection (2), before paragraph (a) there is inserted —
                    "(za)   Strategic Health Authorities,", and
            (b)   after subsection (3) there is inserted —

                    "(4)   Subsection (5) applies to health services for which a Strategic Health Authority is not responsible by virtue of subsection (3), but which are provided or to be provided to individuals in the area of the Authority, and for which —
                            (a)   a Primary Care Trust any part of whose area falls within the Authority's area, or
                            (b)   an NHS trust which provides services at or from a hospital or other establishment or facility which falls within the Authority's area,
                    is responsible by virtue of subsection (3).

                    (5)   A Strategic Health Authority may give directions to Primary Care Trusts falling within paragraph (a) of subsection (4), and NHS trusts falling within paragraph (b) of that subsection, as to the arrangements which they are to make under subsection (1) in relation to health services to which this subsection applies.

                    (6)   It is the duty of each Primary Care Trust and each NHS trust to which such directions are given to comply with them."

36   In section 43 (remote provision of pharmaceutical, etc, services), subsection (5) is omitted.

37   In Schedule 5 (minor and consequential amendments), paragraph 5(12)(b) is omitted.

National Health Service Reform and Health Care Professions Act 2002 (c. 17)
Schedule 9 – Repeals
Part 1 – National Health Service

99

SCHEDULE 9

Section 37(2)

REPEALS

PART 1

NATIONAL HEALTH SERVICE

Short title and chapter	Extent of repeal
Health Services and Public Health Act 1968 (c. 46)	In section 63(5B), the "and" at the end of paragraph (bb).
National Health Service Act 1977 (c. 49)	In section 17B(1), the words from "which" to the end. Section 18(1A)(b). In section 22(1A), the "or" at the end of paragraph (c). In section 28A(1), the "and" at the end of paragraph (a). In section 29B(3), the "or" at the end of paragraph (b). In section 33(1A)(b), "for areas in Wales". In section 44(2), "with the approval of the Health Authority". In section 51(3), the "and" at the end of paragraph (bb). Section 97(6)(bb) and (c) and (8). In section 103(3)(a), "or a Primary Care Trust". In section 125, the "and" at the end of paragraph (bb). In section 126(4A), the "or" at the end of paragraph (b). In Schedule 12A, in paragraph 4(2) the "or" at the end of paragraph (a); in paragraph 5(1) the "and" at the end of paragraph (a); in paragraph 5(2) the "or" at the end of paragraph (a); and in paragraph 7(3) "or Primary Care Trust".
Acquisition of Land Act 1981 (c. 67)	In section 16(3), the "and" at the end of paragraph (b).
Health Service Commissioners Act 1993 (c. 46)	In section 2, in subsection (1)(da), "established for areas in England"; and in subsection (2)(a), "whose areas are in Wales".
Government of Wales Act 1998 (c. 38)	In Schedule 5, in paragraph 20, "for an area in, or consisting of, Wales". In Schedule 17, in paragraph 12, "for an area in, or consisting of, Wales".
Health Act 1999 (c. 8)	In section 6(2), in the inserted section 28EE of the 1977 Act, subsection (1). In section 20(1), the "and" at the end of paragraph (d). In section 23(6), the definition of "NHS premises". In Schedule 2, in paragraph 7(2), the words after "Commission"; and paragraph 7(6) and (7).

100   *National Health Service Reform and Health Care Professions Act 2002 (c. 17)*
Schedule 9 – Repeals
Part 2 – Health care professions

Short title and chapter	Extent of repeal
Health and Social Care Act 2001 (c. 15)	In section 28(7), "or a Primary Care Trust". In Schedule 3, in the new Schedule 8A inserted by that Schedule, in paragraph 1(8), "or a Primary Care Trust".
National Health Service Reform and Health Care Professions Act 2002 (c. 17)	In Schedule 2, in paragraph 2, sub-paragraphs (3) to (5); and paragraph 55.

PART 2

HEALTH CARE PROFESSIONS

Short title and chapter	Extent of repeal
Medical Act 1983 (c. 54)	Section 40(1)(c), (4) to (6), (9) and (10). In Schedule 4, in paragraph 3(b) "to Her Majesty in Council"; paragraph 10(2); in paragraph 10(3) "or (2)", and "or that sub-paragraph as applied by sub-paragraph (2) above". In Schedule 6, in paragraph 18, "section 40(4) of this Act or".
Dentists Act 1984 (c. 24)	Section 29(2). In section 51, the words from "(other" to "appeals)".
Osteopaths Act 1993 (c. 21)	Section 10 (10). Section 31(3) to (5) and (7). Section 35(3).
Chiropractors Act 1994 (c. 17)	Section 10(10). Section 31(3) to (5) and (7). Section 35(3).

PART 3

MISCELLANEOUS

Short title and chapter	Extent of repeal
National Health Service Act 1977 (c. 49)	In section 97D(1)(b), ", apart from subsection (5A)".
National Health Service and Community Care Act 1990 (c. 19)	In section 12(4), the words after paragraph (b).
Local Government (Wales) Act 1994 (c. 19)	In Schedule 10, paragraph 11(4).
Health Authorities Act 1995 (c. 17)	Section 1. In Schedule 1, paragraphs 32(b), 53 and 107(12)(b).
National Health Service (Primary Care) Act 1997 (c. 46)	In Schedule 2, paragraphs 71(3), 73 and 75.

National Health Service Reform and Health Care Professions Act 2002 (c. 17)
Schedule 9 – Repeals
Part 3 – Miscellaneous

101

Short title and chapter	Extent of repeal
Government of Wales Act 1998 (c. 38)	Section 148.
Health Act 1999 (c. 8)	In Schedule 4, paragraphs 5, 31(2) and 35.
Health and Social Care Act 2001 (c. 15)	Section 1(4) and (5). Section 3(3) and (4). Section 43(5). In Schedule 5, paragraph 5(12)(b).

© Crown copyright 2002

Printed in the UK by The Stationery Office Limited
under the authority and superintendence of Carol Tullo, Controller of
Her Majesty's Stationery Office and Queen's Printer of Acts of Parliament